KARL MARX'S

DAS
KAPITAL

KARL MARX'S

DAS KAPITAL

A MODERN-DAY INTERPRETATION
OF AN ECONOMIC CLASSIC
BY STEVE SHIPSIDE

Copyright © Infinite Ideas Limited, 2009
The right of Steve Shipside to be identified as the author of this book has been
asserted in accordance with the Copyright, Designs and Patents Act 1988.

First published in 2009 by
Infinite Ideas Limited
36 St Giles
Oxford, OX1 3LD
United Kingdom
www.infideas.com

A CIP catalogue record for this book is available from the British Library

ISBN 978–1–906821–04–3

Designed and typeset by Cylinder
Printed in India

BRILLIANT IDEAS

INTRODUCTION

On the face of it there's something particularly perverse about writing a modern business ideas book based on an interpretation of Karl Marx. This is, after all, the man who wrote the Communist Manifesto, the man whose only interest in penning *Das Kapital* was to expose the workings of the capitalist system and its pitiless, unsustainable nature in exploiting the working man.

Marx believed that the capitalist system carried the seed of its own doom and would inevitably implode precisely because it was so grossly unfair. He was convinced that not only was a worker's revolution the wholly desirable consequence of capitalism but also an unavoidable one. On this basis the only real interpretation of Kapital would seem to be to burn the building down to go and strike heroic poses in the street with a sledgehammer.

There again, this is the man who said of himself that he was no Marxist. Our understanding of him is inevitably coloured by the interpretation of others and in particular a number of grim, grey regimes and the cant-spouting acolytes they churned out. When you go back to the original, the over-riding impression is of an observer and thinker who is appalled by the hardship suffered by workers, and deeply concerned about perpetuating the system that makes it happen. It's striking just how many of his observations and concerns are every bit as valid now as they were in the 1860s. Marx wasn't just the founding father of communism – he can equally be seen as one of the forefathers of the much more recent, far more trendy, and thoroughly more attractive school of anti-globalisation. He was in no doubt that the workers of the world are not only chained, but linked to each other by those chains. As such, he anticipated the growing concern that we haven't removed the misery of worker exploitation – we've just shipped it over the horizon where we don't actually have to look at it any more. Marx's reflections on sustainable and unsustainable capitalism could just as easily be taken as the starting points for modern business concerns such as ethical consumerism, corporate social responsibility and Fairtrade. The fact that he points out the cyclical nature of capitalism with its boom and bust is particularly interesting reading today, and his documenting of the greed of bankers and the smoke and mirrors of stock markets has special resonance in the light of the credit crunch of 2008–9.

What the modern business commentator knows that Marx didn't, however, was that capitalism wasn't about to implode at the turn of the twentieth century. Instead, some elements of capitalism have recognised its downside and a different, newer way of managing people, resources and exchange has sprung up. This book looks at the concerns of Karl Marx in the light of today's troubles, and suggests some of the alternatives to revolution that have sprung up to deal with the injustice of the system. It is aimed at the modern businessperson who likes to think a little laterally, who is probably involved in some way with the management of people and has a sense of responsibility for that. But it also recognises, as Marx did, that every worker is also a person and as such should be encouraged to develop individually and creatively – without exploiting the others, whose lives they in turn impact upon.

1 SHE'S BREAKING UP, CAPTAIN – UNSUSTAINABLE CAPITALISM

'The monopoly of capital becomes a fetter upon the mode of production, which has sprung up and flourished along with, and under it. Centralisation of the means of production and socialisation of labour at last reach a point where they become incompatible with their capitalist integument... The knell of capitalist private property sounds.'

DEFINING IDEA...

Sir Isaac Newton was asked about the continuance of the rising of South Sea stock... He answered that he 'could not calculate the madness of people'.

~ LORD RADNOR

Marx's apocalyptic language reflects his conviction that the seeds of capitalism's downfall are to be found in its core – basically the whole system will accelerate to a pitch where capitalism eats itself. If that sounds melodramatic, bear in mind that the 2009 economic downturn has revealed that the cutting edge of capitalism has become the packaging up and selling on of bad debt. If that's not capitalism eating itself, it's hard to imagine what is.

Sub-prime mortgages and junk bonds may be recent twists to the tale but Marx was more than familiar with the absurdities of untrammelled capitalism – in 1719, the South Sea Company proposed a scheme by which it would buy more than half the national debt of Britain. That triggered a share spike in which a rash of unsound companies rushed to market, but by 1720 all these schemes had collapsed – but capitalism's appetite for the unfeasible is clearly undiminished.

'Profits are for wimps' was the famous motto of Jeff Bezos, CEO of Amazon at the height of the dot-com boom at the end of the nineties. When the dot-com boom turned into the dot-bomb collapse, financial markets ruefully reminded each other that profits are actually for shareholders and a financial model based on no product at all is always a bubble ripe for bursting. The sub-prime scandal followed in less than a decade. At the time of writing, the financial world is still reeling from the $50 billion scam pulled off by Wall Street broker Bernard Madoff. That has rapidly been denounced as a classic pyramid scheme in which the whole edifice stands on the shoulders of new punters who are brought in with their money. The key point of a pyramid scheme is that at its heart there is a void rather than a genuine product. Nothing at all, therefore, like those perfectly legitimate financial transactions in which unrecoverable debt is traded from one bank to another for ever-increasing amounts of money.

Of course, a pure capitalist might argue that the failure of the system is that it is not sufficiently untrammelled and that banks should not be bailed out by governments when they fail but instead allowed to go to the wall. The impact of that on individuals and societies affected by it, however, means we can't do that and must recognise the social impact of capitalism. Which means guarding against unsustainable forms of capitalism and instead building sustainability (including social sustainability) into the system – as we shall see in the next few chapters.

HERE'S AN IDEA FOR YOU...

The key to bubbles is that the value set on the investments was based on a rush of enthusiasm. Sometimes that works, but rarely for long – and those who don't leave in time will get burnt. Audit your investments, personal and corporate, and consider which depend on a short-term effect for their appeal.

2 SUSTAINABLE CAPITALISM

'The capitalist mode of appropriation, the result of the capitalist mode of production, produces capitalist private property. This is the first negation of individual private property, as founded on the labour of the proprietor. But capitalist production begets, with the inexorability of a law of Nature, its own negation. It is the negation of negation.'

DEFINING IDEA...

We have to choose between a global market driven only by calculation of short-term profit, and one which has a human face.
– KOFI ANNAN

Marx believed that capitalism would go out in a ball of flames, consumed by itself and overthrown by an inevitable proletariat backlash which would see the means of production restored to the worker. What he didn't predict was that capitalism's excesses might then trigger a backlash among capitalists and consumers, who would then begin to clamour for a more caring form of capitalism – one that took pains to protect the people and even build a better world. Nor would Marx necessarily have approved; as much as he would have been happy to see improvements in living standards and ethical approaches, he would probably have seen these as sticking plasters to slow a moral decay which he would have preferred to build momentum until it crashed and burned.

Whatever he would have made of it, the fact is that modern business ignores the issues of sustainability and social responsibility at its peril. You don't have to have a tendency to hug trees to see why – even the most jaded corporate cynic can see that bringing an ethical dimension to trade and doing business with a sense of social responsibility is increasingly a prerequisite, and one with positive paybacks. In an age of increased consumer and media awareness (and the advent of the Web has made the two all but interchangeable) a business that operates in a purely 'red in tooth and claw' manner runs the risk of losing business partners, business boycotts, lawsuits, loss of employees, the unwanted attentions of advocacy groups, negative press or PR and even legislation.

In Marx's time very few of these were really a threat for big business, especially if they had the delicacy to commit the worst of their brutishness out of sight and sound. Back in 1867 that was easily enough done, since the poor and oppressed had no effective voice. The uneducated workers were easy to divide and conquer and anything done in far-away lands tended to stay there as long as the profits made it back home.

'Social responsibility' takes in a wide remit, but as a general guide it can be broken down into seven key areas: financial responsibility, ethics, diversity, community, environment, human rights and safety.

Marx might not have approved of any steps that would help prop up the capitalist system, but it's clear from *Das Kapital* that each of the above would have been priorities in his own view of how the worker's lot should be improved. You don't have to live in fear of the proletariat rising up and taking control of the factories to implement socially responsible business models; these days responsible business is simply good business.

HERE'S AN IDEA FOR YOU...

Social responsibility is a feel-good term with no concrete meaning, right? Wrong. Not only is there a forthcoming ISO standard on social responsibility, but there are tools to help you assess and act on it. Try the Institute For Supply Management (ISM) and its Responsibility Prioritization Tool to analyse where your business could benefit.

3 ETHICS

'Political Economy, which as an independent science first sprang into being during the period of manufacture, views the social division of labour only from the standpoint of manufacture, and sees in it only the means of producing more commodities with a given quantity of labour, and, consequently, of cheapening commodities and hurrying on the accumulation of capital.'

DEFINING IDEA...

In law a man is guilty when he violates the rights of others. In ethics he is guilty if he only thinks of doing so.

~ IMMANUEL KANT

Do you know how many times Karl Marx uses the word 'ethics' in his analysis of capital and the development of industrialism? Not once. That's a sign of the times in itself, since no business report now is complete without at least some token examination of the issue of business ethics. In Marx's time the phrase 'business ethics' was probably little used and, besides, his whole point about the modern 'science' of political economy is that it has no ethical side at all – it is by nature uncaring and dehumanising.

When business is booming ethics seem irrelevant. When times are hard they can seem unaffordable. Marx would have said that this was due to the nature of capitalism itself and its basis in the (often brutal) exploitation of the working man. These days, however, there's a growing argument that exploitation is not a sustainable business model and a more ethical approach to business is essential for long term success.

The UK Institute of Business Ethics suggests a simple 'test' for ethical decision-making in business. Essentially it proposes that the next time you (or you as the representative of your company) have to make a judgement call, you first consider the ethical trilogy of Transparency, Effect and Fairness. It would be nice if those three combined to a snappy acronym but they don't (TEF? EFT? FET? I give up).

What they mean is…
- Transparency – what would I feel if this decision (and my part in it) was made public?
- Effect – am I sure that I've taken into account (and tried to avoid) any harmful effects my decision could have?
- Fairness – would everyone affected, directly or indirectly, consider that I'd acted in a fair way (even if they didn't agree with the decision)?

Life being what it is, you'd be lucky to find the answer was 'yes' to all of the above any time you were having a hard time making a decision. If you're not sure, then this may be your cue to take some advice from someone else. Clearly that should be someone with a strong ethical guiding principle, rather than an interested party. Remember you have to include the third party in your original three questions, so if you were thinking of going to the fox to ask for advice about the chickens you're likely to fall foul of all three rules just by doing so. Now let other people in on the secret of your personal ethical threesome – wouldn't you rather that anyone with influence on your life lived by that trio? Well, so would those who depend on you.

HERE'S AN IDEA FOR YOU…

Come up with a company Code of Ethics. This gives employees a standard to work to and a suggestion of criteria to apply when decisions aren't clear cut. Of course, your ethical code is worth precisely zip if you don't apply it or it's blatant bluff. That includes woolly admonitions such as 'Don't be Evil' (Google's watchword).

4 CAN CAPITALISM AFFORD A CONSCIENCE?

'As the conscious representative of this movement, the possessor of money becomes a capitalist. His person, or rather his pocket, is the point from which the money starts and to which it returns...and it is only in so far as the appropriation of ever more and more wealth in the abstract becomes the sole motive of his operations, that he functions as a capitalist, that is, as capital personified and endowed with consciousness and a will.'

DEFINING IDEA...

How wonderful it is that nobody need wait a single moment before starting to improve the world.

– ANNE FRANK

Pure capitalism is driven only by the appropriation of wealth, and from his observations of the grasping capitalism of the nineteenth century Marx saw the capitalist's consciousness and will to be completely at the service of the amassing of money. These days, however, the idea of capitalism with a conscience has evolved for a number of key reasons. Firstly, the idea of a company having responsibility has emerged as a rebuke to the excesses of capitalism. Secondly, it's been shown that a corporate conscience can help boost the bottom line; thirdly, there is plenty of pressure to pay lip service to the idea – even by companies so greedy they'd have made Marx's mill owners blush.

In the introduction to the ISM (the Institute For Supply Management) Principles of Social Responsibility, Paul Novak, CEO of ISM, observes that 'Commitment to socially responsible behaviour is good business – in both the public and private sectors. Often payback can be quantified in financial terms. Socially responsible behaviour may even ensure that an enterprise will avoid difficult or embarrassing scrutiny. However, "soft" payback in dignity, success, self-worth and honour provides the real foundation and rationale for socially responsible behaviour.'

Soft payback is hard to quantify, and given the choice between honour and hard cash a lot of shareholders would quietly take the cash. The catch is that these days it's getting harder to pocket ill-gotten gains without someone noticing and blowing the whistle. Business has not always succeeded in regulating itself, as was made evident by a number of corporate accounting scandals in the early noughties. In the US the law felt forced to step in and the best known result to date has been the Sarbanes–Oxley Act of 2002, commonly called Sarbanes–Oxley, Sarbox or SOX.

SOX is principally concerned with avoiding accounting scandals but in the process it demands increased transparency with accountability for actions taken by directors in a corporation. That, however, has not only made it harder for senior management to pinch the petty cash, it has also opened up the ethical stances of companies to inspection by peers, punters and the press. In Marx's day big business was all but unaccountable, but the over-reaching greed of a few capitalists may have done the entire business world a favour by forcibly installing the idea of legal accountability. Capitalism is a long way from being on the straight and narrow, but at least it has an institutional Jiminy Cricket perched on its shoulder.

HERE'S AN IDEA FOR YOU...

Appoint an Ethics Officer. They've been around since the 1980s as a personification of company conscience and/or a sop to shareholders – depending on your cynicism level. It doesn't have to be full time, but by making someone a moral barometer you increase the recognition of the importance of responsibility.

5 TRIPLE BOTTOM LINE

'The discovery of gold and silver in America, the extirpation, enslavement and entombment in mines of the aboriginal population, the beginning of the conquest and looting of the East Indies, the turning of Africa into a warren for the commercial hunting of black-skins, signalised the rosy dawn of the era of capitalist production. These idyllic proceedings are the chief momenta of primitive accumulation.'

DEFINING IDEA...

The world won't tolerate businesses that don't take that partnership seriously, but it will eventually reward companies that do.

– C. MICHAEL ARMSTRONG, CHAIRMAN AND CEO, AT&T

Marx was under no illusions about the capitalist exploitation of the planet and its peoples, and there is no shortage of examples of the same process today. Blood wars wage in Africa over diamonds; the rights of local people come a poor second to the quest for fuel, and where minerals occur in marine reserves it seems there's always an unscrupulous politician happy to sell extraction rights. The heavy sarcasm Marx reserves for these 'idyllic proceedings' hints at his world weariness and would be equally appropriate now.

It doesn't have to be that way. Increasingly there is a trend for companies to talk about the Triple Bottom Line (aka TBL or 3BL). Triple Bottom Line accounting means broadening the traditional financial reporting framework to incorporate ecological and social performance. At its heart is the idea that a company is not simply responsible to its shareholders, but to its stakeholders – anyone whose life is influenced by the actions of that company. TBL is also sometimes known as the Three Ps – people, planet, profit.

People, in this case, means fair business practices aimed at benefiting the community affected by the business. Fairtrade-certified commodities, for example, not only take into account a fair price for small producers, but also assure standards of worker care.

Planet means sustainable environmental practices and a reduced footprint. You don't have to be a logging company in the rainforest to have a huge impact on the environment; every office – even those with no physical product – is a massive consumer of power, petrochemical-based plastics, chemicals and packaging.

Profit is the bottom line and considers not just the immediate benefits to the company but also the longer-term economic impact on its market. This can also prove good business sense, as it emphasises that a short-term scramble for a niche market must be weighed against long-term sustainability.

The Triple Bottom Line approach has also become big business in certain industries. Note the growth of eco-tourism, for example, the success of which is based entirely on the approach. Marx would have been surprised by the development of TBL, but then he could hardly have foreseen the development of mass media and, in particular, the World Wide Web with its ability to generate and host debate while also allowing even niche companies to reach a wider public. It's hard to say if he would have approved. The emphasis on community is classically Marxist, but he might have suspected that it was another sticking plaster on the gaping wounds of a deeply flawed system. It would be nice to prove him wrong.

HERE'S AN IDEA FOR YOU...

Fire up a spreadsheet and start to create a template for Triple Bottom Line reporting in your company. What categories would you have to include in the 'people' and 'planet' parts of the equation? What is the scale of your company's impact? When it comes to green economics, is your company in the red or the black?

6 MARKET FAILURE AND THE ENVIRONMENT

'Capital cares nothing for the length of life of labour-power. All that concerns it is simply and solely the maximum of labour-power, that can be rendered fluent in a working-day. It attains this end by shortening the extent of the labourer's life, as a greedy farmer snatches increased produce from the soil by robbing it of its fertility.'

DEFINING IDEA...

You can uphold human rights and decent labour and environmental standards directly, by your own conduct of your own business.

– KOFI ANNAN

It's no accident that Karl compares the abuse of workers with the exploitation of the soil. What he saw happening around him had subjugated both these processes to the principle of amassing the maximum capital. In doing so, he also points to one of the biggest failings of the capitalist system. Quite simply, it is a remarkable and largely self-regulating means of establishing markets – of trading off supply and demand and ensuring a global movement of produce and wealth. What it doesn't do at all, however, is make any allowance for those things that can't be totted up in traditional profit and loss accounting, such as the damage to ecosystems or even the carrying capacity of the entire planet. Marx doesn't feel the need to explain why the greedy farmer is short-sighted and stupid. He doesn't go into the cycle of nitrogen fixing, of leaving land fallow, or applying fertiliser. He simply presumes that his reader instantly sees why the farmer is ultimately robbing not just the soil but also himself by failing to put anything back. Pure capitalism might argue that the farmer in question will be forced to see the error of his ways because sooner or later his crops will start to fail and his land will become worthless unless he adopts a more sustainable approach. The market will enforce a correction in this case.

The problem is that on the larger scale of global markets the damage done is rarely so closely linked to the cause and so the case for correction is lost. Markets can fail to work sustainably for a number of reasons. The sheer scale may mean that we are not aware of the amount of depletion. Can you picture the size of a rainforest? In 2005 the UN declared that 13 million hectares of forest are lost each year, but what does that mean to you or me when we're standing in a furniture shop? Then there is the problem that the link between cause and effect is obscured by distance – I have never been to the Mato Grosso in Brazil and even if I went it would be hard to see how my shiny new table had impacted on its biodiversity. Then there's the problem that capitalism tends to privatise natural capital to exploit it, but the real costs are externalised as a problem for society in general.

In short, capitalism does a great job of reaping the profit but when it comes to cleaning up it's nowhere to be seen. Unlike the foolish farmer in Marx's story, global capitalism can always move on. At least until the planet is sucked dry.

HERE'S AN IDEA FOR YOU...

We love to recycle (who'd have thought such a small gesture could save the planet?) but if you're really concerned, the big savings come when entire companies get in on the act. Who is responsible for the audit of your company's environmental impact? Nobody? Then maybe it's time to step forward.

7 ENVIRONMENTAL ECONOMICS

'The soil (and this, economically speaking, includes water) in the virgin state in which it supplies man with necessaries or the means of subsistence ready to hand, exists independently of him, and is the universal subject of human labour. All those things which labour merely separates from immediate connexion with their environment, are subjects of labour spontaneously provided by Nature. Such are fish which we catch and take from their element, water, timber which we fell in the virgin forest, and ores which we extract from their veins.'

DEFINING IDEA...

A pirate throwing a few doubloons to a beggar may claim to be a philanthropist, but that hardly makes him a responsible businessman.

– LORD HOLME, RIO TINTO

Back in the 1860s, environmental awareness wasn't the headline-grabber it is today and Marx only really touches on the issue of the environment as a form of natural capital which the worker is (you guessed it) alienated from by the capitalist system and the division of labour. These days, however, there is a growing understanding that far from having a never-ending supply of raw materials, the planet may actually be running out. In Marx's day it was unthinkable that cod might become too scarce to catch and countries could lose up to three quarters of their forests; now those are facts of life. Since money makes the world go around the pressure is on to come up with a business case for sustainable development.

The World Business Council for Sustainable Development (WBCSD) defined eco-efficiency back in the 90s when it declared that 'Eco-efficiency is achieved by the delivery of competitively-priced goods and services that satisfy human needs and bring quality of life, while progressively reducing ecological impacts and resource intensity throughout the life-cycle to a level at least in line with the earth's carrying capacity.'

The carrying capacity means its ability to support the more demanding species (that would be us). If we exploit unsustainably then resources begin to run out, reducing the planet's ability to sustain our population. Eco-efficiency aims to avoid that by calculating the economic value added by a company in relation to the ecological impact it has as a result of its operation. Much of *Das Kapital* is about the conversion of one form of capital into another. Labour is converted into wages which are in turn converted into the buying of goods which are themselves the product of labour, etc. What Marx didn't include was the concept that some capital might not be so simply converted into another and might not be infinite. No amount of money will bring back an extinct species, and it remains to be seen if the ozone layer can be repaired.

Marx's particular focus was on the analysis of causal links between consumption, labour, capital, and currency. The point of *Das Kapital* was to expose the way in which they were interlinked and show that the system was founded on the exploitation of the worker. The equivalent move now is, firstly, to establish the causality between business and finite natural resources and, secondly, to get business and government alike to take responsibility for accounting for those resources.

HERE'S AN IDEA FOR YOU...

Monitoring the planet isn't easy, but there are tools available to help build a picture of the complex relationships between economic, social, and environmental issues. Take a look at the Dashboard of Sustainability at http://esl.jrc.it/envind/dashbrds.htm – it's free of charge and can be customised by importing data from your own spreadsheets.

8 YOU NEED TO GET OUT MORE, MATE

'Co-operation, such as we find it at the dawn of human development, among races who live by the chase, or, say, in the agriculture of Indian communities, is based, on the one hand, on ownership in common of the means of production, and on the other hand, on the fact, that in those cases, each individual has no more torn himself off from the navel-string of his tribe or community, than each bee has freed itself from connexion with the hive.'

DEFINING IDEA...

The individual is helpless socially, if left to himself...
– L. HANIFAN

In the struggle to find a better form of capitalism, the concept of social capital is increasingly finding favour. Marx touches on the bottom line of social capital above when he talks about the navel-string of tribe and community – a sense of connection with the hive. The phrase 'social capital' itself is often accredited to L. Hanifan, a schools supervisor in the US in 1916 who defined social capital as 'those tangible substances [that] count for most in the daily lives of people: namely good will, fellowship, sympathy, and social intercourse among the individuals and families who make up a social unit'.

Marx's point is that capitalism has alienated workers from their role in a traditional (and relatively small) community, and set them adrift in the industrial cities. It's a concern that endures and can be found expressed in such works as Bowling Alone: America's Declining Social Capital by Professor Robert Putnam (1995). Here the good prof examines US society since 1950 in terms of participation in public meetings, political parties and voter turn-out. His conclusion is that society is withdrawing from civic engagement and turning in on itself, something he attributes partly to TV and home entertainment.

The point of social capital is that it is of benefit to all concerned – that each transaction enriches both parties and builds relationships, trust and a network of contacts that increases society's productivity. Networking in the sense of building business contacts is perhaps the most obvious manifestation of that, but the word-of-mouth sourcing of products, jobs and help in tightly-knit communities goes beyond simply social climbing or smoothing your way into influence. In short, if you want to get on you need to get out more.

Different cultures have different attitudes to mixing – English city dwellers, for example, are notorious for barely knowing their neighbours. That doesn't stop us from going out and forming bonds. There are any number of places to increase your social capital by meeting up with like-minded people – that doesn't just mean political organisations or 'self help societies'. Running groups, book clubs, crèches, even diet clubs are all ways of hooking up with people you may find you have a lot in common with. Marx would see this as a means of combating the alienation of the ordinary man in a capitalist society. Perhaps it is; certainly, it's a lot easier and a great deal less dangerous than arming yourself and rushing on to the streets with a view to forcibly re-taking the means of production.

HERE'S AN IDEA FOR YOU...

TV and computers may have made people more introspective, but the Net has given us online communities. While there may be hours of fun to be had on Facebook, there are also more serious communities being built to connect businesspeople. Try joining LinkedIn and build contact networks of past, current and possibly future colleagues.

9 CAREFUL WITH THAT AXE, EUGENE – LUDDITISM

'In the 17th century nearly all Europe experienced revolts of the workpeople against the ribbon-loom, a machine for weaving ribbons and trimmings, called in Germany Bandmühle, Schnurmühle, and Mühlenstuhl.' We refer to rebels against the machine as Luddites, but that may be simply because 'Ned Ludd' is easier to pronounce than 'Schnurmühle'.

DEFINING IDEA...

All business sagacity reduces itself in the last analysis to judicious use of sabotage.

~ THORSTEIN VEBLEN,
AMERICAN ECONOMIST

Marx records that as early as 1579 there was an ingenious machine which wove four to six pieces of ribbon at once – 'But the Mayor being apprehensive that this invention might throw a large number of workmen on the streets, caused the inventor to be secretly strangled or drowned.

In Leyden, this machine was not used till 1629; there the riots of the ribbon-weavers at length compelled the Town Council to prohibit it.'

Life, it seems, was positively dangerous for inventors in the dawn of the industrial revolution. It was a pattern that was to be repeated: 'About 1630, a wind-sawmill, erected near London by a Dutchman, succumbed to the excesses of the populace. Even as late as the beginning of the 18th century, sawmills driven by water overcame the opposition of the people, supported as it was by Parliament, only with great difficulty. No sooner had Everet in 1758 erected the first wool-shearing machine that was driven by water-power, than it was set on fire by 100,000 people who had been thrown out of work.'

New technology was feared, despised, and set upon even before the organised sabotage of Ned Ludd and the Luddite movement. 'It took both time and experience before the workpeople learnt to distinguish between machinery and its employment by capital, and to direct their attacks, not against the material instruments of production, but against the mode in which they are used.' Here Karl was a little optimistic. Modern day Luddites have yet to learn to make that distinction and frequently live in horror and loathing of the technology which they are given to help make their own lives easier.

Modern Luddites don't usually smash and burn their computers (though we've all dreamt of doing it) but they may well sabotage projects and innovations by silent resistance or deeply grudging acceptance. Managing change doesn't usually come with the risk of being 'secretly strangled or drowned' but it does remain a delicate affair if you want to make progress. In many cases new technologies or practices are simply presented to the workforce with the assumption that the workers will either immediately appreciate their benefits or appreciate the idea that they have to evolve or become redundant. Whilst this 'learn or die' approach can be remarkably effective, it is also just as likely to foster resentment – which combines neatly with people's fear of the new to create resistance to the innovation.

HERE'S AN IDEA FOR YOU...

No matter how obvious the benefits of a new approach seem to you, don't spring it on your staff without a clearly laid-out phase of consultation and progressive implementation. Try appointing Change Stewards – stakeholders amongst the staff who stand to gain. Change effected from within is far more likely to endure.

10 TECHNOTOPIA

'The machine proper is…a mechanism that, after being set in motion, performs with its tools the same operations that were formerly done by the workman with similar tools.' Marx's definition of technology was, ahem, just a little vague…

DEFINING IDEA…

When capital enlists science into her service, the refractory hand of labour will always be taught docility.

– ANDREW URE, AUTHOR OF PHILOSOPHY OF MANUFACTURES FROM 1835, TALKING ABOUT THE 'MULE' MACHINE

The argument rages over whether Marx was a technological determinist (the belief that technology determines a society's cultural values) or not, but it seems fair to say that he was caught up between the two competing promises of technology. On the one hand, technology was busy changing the nature of society in his time – not for the better – whilst on the other he also saw technology as a powerful force for change, able to empower mankind and in the process undermine monarchies and the power of the church.

Marx was a keen-eyed observer of industrial history and noted that while machines could bring great progress, the way they were implemented could equally bring great trauma: 'When machinery seizes on an industry by degrees, it produces chronic misery among the operatives who compete with it. Where the transition is rapid, the effect is acute and felt by great masses.' You could argue that Karl was an early technorealist – someone occupying the middle ground between the techno-utopians, who felt that science was the saving of mankind, and the neo-Luddites who set out to oppose technology.

Or you could just say that the beardy boy was a realist who was as aware of the cruelty and unjustness that sprang from technology as he was of its promise.

What matters in the modern context is that the pace of technological change may have accelerated to warp speed but the polarity of responses remains the same. Technorealism is by far the most balanced approach, particularly in difficult times when the cost-saving (and labour force-saving) benefits of new technology tend to be promoted ahead of less easily quantified benefits such as improved individual productivity or new working patterns. Take the shifting patterns of call centres. Initially the call centre largely created jobs that hadn't previously existed, since few companies employed enough staff at head office to handle full-on customer interaction. Marx wouldn't have foreseen that, since he mainly saw technology removing jobs. Areas such as Scotland and Ireland immediately benefited.

As Internet technology began to handle the routing of calls and it cost much the same to re-route calls to the other side of the earth, a flurry of companies moved their call centres offshore and saved a fortune in the process. Marx would have pointed to that as an example of the technology causing chronic misery among the operatives. A more technorealist approach is now appearing as the limitations of foreign call centres are felt by consumers. Some functions are now coming home due, in part, to the ability to create 'virtual' call centres with part-time or flexible workers logging on from home. That may not save the company as much money as a full-blown Mumbai call centre, but for certain operations it pays off in customer satisfaction.

HERE'S AN IDEA FOR YOU...

If you're looking at new systems in a credit crunch, the trick is to focus as much on the potential for boosting productivity as lowering outgoings. That way your business is ready to re-expand once the crunch passes, rather than having 'streamlined' itself into a corner.

11 CHILD LABOUR

'In so far as machinery dispenses with muscular power, it becomes a means of employing labourers of slight muscular strength, and those whose bodily development is incomplete, but whose limbs are all the more supple. The labour of women and children was, therefore, the first thing sought for by capitalists who used machinery.'

The industrial revolution may be history now, but Marx's concern about child labour is every bit as relevant today.

DEFINING IDEA…

The worst thief is he who steals the playtime of children!

– BILL HAYWOOD, LEADER OF THE INDUSTRIAL WORKERS OF THE WORLD UNION

Machinery effectively replaces the need for physical strength, and with it the reliance on men as labourers. Marx also noted that the textile industries – then the cutting edge of mechanisation – better suited the smaller, more nimble hands of women and children. 'Previously, the workman sold his own labour-power, which he disposed of nominally as a free agent. Now he sells wife and child. He has become a slave-dealer.'

Melodramatic as this may sound, Marx went into some detail to make his point: 'The demand for children's labour often resembles in form the inquiries for negro slaves, such as were formerly to be read among the advertisements in American journals.' He quotes factory inspectors scouring newspaper adverts looking for workers '…not younger than what can pass for 13 years'. The significance of this was that under the Factory Act children below that age were limited in the hours they could work. The factories weren't interested in the real age; just that they could get away with the argument that they themselves had been duped by underage workers.

Little has changed. When Nike was caught employing child labour in Cambodia, the company's response was that fake evidence of age could be bought in Cambodia for as little as $5.

Marx tells of a twice-weekly market in Bethnal Green where '…children of both sexes from 9 years of age upwards, hire themselves out to the silk manufacturers. The usual terms are 1s. 8d. a week (this belongs to the parents) and "2d. for myself and tea." The contract is binding only for the week. The scene and language while this market is going on are quite disgraceful.' Nike was accused of exploiting workers as young as ten in the making of footballs. Human rights groups claim that Nike continues to source labour in parts of the world where regulation of child labour is hard to enforce. Despite strenuous denials by the company, there is ongoing criticism in the media.

Aside from the moral issues involved, there is no doubt that the slightest suspicion of child exploitation means PR death. Nike has been dogged by the subject not because it's the only company to do it, but because its branding revolves around the idea of empowerment and youth. Similarly, when whiter-than-white talk show hostess Kathie Lee Gifford – an ambassador for the charity Childhelp – was accused of using child labour in a Honduras sweatshop where her clothing line was made, her career nearly ended. Such brands need to go the extra mile, and enforce standards over and above those expected of others.

HERE'S AN IDEA FOR YOU…

Initiate a supplier scorecard with age criteria for workers. Insist on ranking suppliers depending on what precautions they can demonstrate they are taking against the exploitation of minors. Make it clear that business only continues if the scorecard doesn't fall below a given level.

12 BREAKING THE CHAINS – REACHING FOR THE OFF BUTTON

'If machinery be the most powerful means for increasing the productiveness of labour – i.e., for shortening the working-time required in the production of a commodity, it becomes in the hands of capital the most powerful means, in those industries first invaded by it, for lengthening the working-day beyond all bounds set by human nature.'

DEFINING IDEA...

It is questionable if all the mechanical inventions yet made have lightened the day's toil of any human being.
– JOHN STUART MILL, POLITICAL PHILOSOPHER

Substitute the word 'technology' for the word 'machinery' and you'll immediately see that Karl Marx's point remains as valid today as it was in the age of the spinning jenny and the mechanised loom. Labour-saving devices, in the capitalist machinery, aren't intended to make life easier – they're meant to make more money for the owner of the system. In the context of the time Marx was writing this made particular sense, since industrial innovation was largely geared towards increasing individual productivity at the cost of the workforce and to the benefit – and profit – of the mill owner. These days the picture is rather more complex, since the tools for personal productivity also allow the individual more scope to expand their own activities or shape their working lives to fit better with their personal time management.

An Ipsos Reid study for Research In Motion (the makers of the BlackBerry) suggests that a typical working day includes at least 60 minutes of unused time that can be clawed back if we use it productively. That means 250 hours every year – a huge chunk of life given back to you if you took those dead minutes spent in trains, planes and queues and used that time productively instead. Before you rush out to buy a BlackBerry, however, just take a look at the reality of the people who use them (and similar devices). Their digital devices start to pop up in all sorts of previously personal moments. No meal can be eaten without a quick pause to check email. Discussions between friends are conducted with one party (and sometimes both) staring down at a minute keyboard in the palm of the hand. I even know of couples who have had to implement rigid 'no email in the bedroom' rules in order to avoid having their most private moments of the day hijacked by their little productivity devices.

Karl's point wasn't far off the mark back then, and it can still prove surprisingly relevant now. Personal productivity devices are all too often only about improving your productivity for the organisation you work for. It takes a lot of planning and willpower to turn them into the life-enhancing extras that the glossy magazine adverts might lead you to expect. If that wasn't the truth then why would so many corporates be so happy to fork out for 'productivity enhancers' for their senior staff? These days the chains that bind are likely to come with an LCD screen and 3G connectivity, but their grip is no less strangling.

HERE'S AN IDEA FOR YOU...

Impose your own routine on the PDA. Just as you switch off your mobile phone before a film starts in the cinema (you do, don't you?) learn to switch off your handheld device before anything worthy of attention – a conversation, a meeting, a meal, etc. Otherwise you're not increasing your productivity; you're just extending your working hours.

13 TIME MANAGEMENT – LESS IS MORE

'The introduction of the Factory Acts,' notes Marx, *'has strikingly shown that the mere shortening of the working-day increases to a wonderful degree the regularity, uniformity, order, continuity and energy of the labour.'* **In other words, working longer doesn't necessarily bring better rewards – not even for the capitalist overlord.**

DEFINING IDEA...

Dost thou love life? Then do not squander time, for that is the stuff life is made of.

~ BENJAMIN FRANKLIN

Travel around, and you will see some striking differences in work culture. Years ago, I worked for an American publishing company that was launching simultaneously in the UK, France and Germany. The American executives charged with the launch were happy with the London office, where workers ate lunch at their keyboards and rarely left before seven at night. They were flustered by the French who insisted on a two-hour lunch break, and baffled by the Germans who were sticklers for detail, precise timekeeping and leaving bang on time at 5.30.

Satisfying as it is to see national stereotypes being played out in reality, the key point was that each culture had its own way of working. What outsiders so often missed was that the French lunch break was a key part of the working day. Not only did it strengthen the bonds between co-workers (having lunch on your own would have been seen as eccentric at best) but it was often the point at which real business was done – the morning's meetings being a mere pre-amble before the complex processes of negotiation, concession and agreement that would take place between the entrée and the final coffee. Meanwhile, the German insistence on leaving on time was as much a statement about work efficiency as the Anglo-Saxon desk-squatting. Their attitude was that anyone who stayed late was clearly a poor time-manager.

National differences are being eroded by global business and the Anglo-Saxon model is increasingly prevalent, but there's much to be said for the idea of strictly limiting your work hours as a means of both increasing your productivity and reclaiming your life. Working smarter, not harder, should be a personal as well as a professional manifesto. The effect of reducing hours was evident to Karl Marx over a century and a half ago: 'Mr. Robert Gardner reduced the hours of labour in his two large factories at Preston, on and after the 20th April, 1844, from twelve to eleven hours a day. The result of about a year's working was that "the same amount of product for the same cost was received, and the workpeople as a whole earned in eleven hours as much wages as they did before in twelve."' This, according to Marx, was because 'the shortening of the hours of labour creates, to begin with, the subjective conditions for the condensation of labour, by enabling the workman to exert more strength in a given time'.

The same message holds true today (though physical strength may be less of an issue) if we fail to distinguish between hours spent at work and productivity. Better to work fresher, faster and better, than to spend hours at the keyboard – whatever the unspoken peer pressure.

HERE'S AN IDEA FOR YOU...

You think nothing of setting an alarm to ensure you get to work on time, so why not set an alarm to make sure you leave on time? Setting yourself a precise daily deadline means you'll be less likely to allow work to expand and more likely to finish it early.

14 DOLING OUT THE DRUDGE WORK

'The miserable routine of endless drudgery and toil in which the same mechanical process is gone through over and over again, is like the labour of Sisyphus. The burden of labour, like the rock, keeps ever falling back on the worn-out labourer.'

'In manufacture,' says Marx, 'the workmen are parts of a living mechanism. In the factory we have a lifeless mechanism independent of the workman, who becomes its mere living appendage… The lightening of the labour, even, becomes a sort of torture, since the machine does not free the labourer from work, but deprives the work of all interest.'

DEFINING IDEA...

Work is not the curse, drudgery is.

– HENRY WARD BEECHER
US CONGREGATIONAL MINISTER

It's a rare job indeed that doesn't involve a certain amount of drudge work. No matter how glamorous it can be made to sound when you're trying to impress someone else, every line of work – be it working as an airline pilot or as a cabaret artist – entails a certain amount of paperwork and dull routine. The higher you make it up the management ladder, the less that may be the case – but it is still always there and the good manager not only strives to reduce their own drudgery but that of others, since a happy workforce is a more productive one. So how do you prevent that labourer from becoming 'worn-out'? For that matter, how do you stop it happening to yourself?

One potential answer is to stop trying to hand it over and instead institute a sharing system. While everybody resents certain aspects of a job, at least by adopting a rota system they take these in turns and nobody ends up stuck with the less-than-sweet-smelling end of the stick all the time. Another way is to take what might seem to be the opposite approach and see whether the drudge part of the task can be farmed out altogether to a third party. Outsourcing your problems may pay for itself in terms of increased morale, productivity and allowing your more talented staff to focus on what it is that they actually do best. A third way is to look at outsourcing to flexible workers within your own company. Dull or stressful work is more easily handled by those who don't have to wake up to it every day, and may be seen as a worthwhile trade-off in return for the flexible or home working which means that they still earn revenue for a few days work a week.

Whether you go for full-on outsourcing, sourcing to flexible workers or a rota system don't forget that constant monitoring is required to ensure your drudge workers don't suffer from burnout. In the case of remote or outsourced staff, this will need particular attention since you may not be on site to gauge morale. Whatever solution you opt for, try to ensure that nobody feels stuck in a dead end of Sisyphean slavery.

HERE'S AN IDEA FOR YOU...

Form a Dirty Dozen – a team that specialises in the sticky bits and takes pride in it. One online advertising company took the work of producing ad banners (a repetitive task) away from their precious creatives and gave it to a dedicated team who were rewarded with a productivity-linked pay scale. They developed team spirit and specialist pride.

15 SET YOUR MIND FREE FROM THE BOX

Marx was acutely aware of the ability of work to dull the mind. *'As a matter of fact, some few manufacturers in the middle of the 18th century preferred, for certain operations that were trade secrets, to employ half-idiotic persons.'* A fair few modern businesses seem to do the same, just maybe not on purpose.

DEFINING IDEA...

We are all born ignorant, but one must work hard to remain stupid.

~ BENJAMIN FRANKLIN

'In manufacture, in order to make the collective labourer, and through him capital, rich in social productive power, each labourer must be made poor in individual productive powers.' Or, put another way, Marx asserts that in order to better serve as tools for the machine, each labourer must become as witless as any other tool. It's an idea he takes from the eighteenth-century economist Adam Smith whom he quotes at length on the subject: 'Ignorance is the mother of industry as well as of superstition. Reflection and fancy are subject to err; but a habit of moving the hand or the foot is independent of either. Manufactures, accordingly, prosper most where the mind is least consulted, and where the workshop may...be considered as an engine, the parts of which are men.'

These days its unlikely you, good reader, are working on an assembly line, not least since the majority of extraordinarily numbing jobs have been automated or outsourced to Asia (Marx would be bellowing 'I told you so' at this point). That doesn't alter the fact, however, that the machine as such still exists and can still demand we serve it best by subjugating ourselves to its interests. The differences are that, firstly, the machine is more subtle – having become a virtual assembly of ideas, corporate brands and international markets – and, secondly, the workers are more cynical since company loyalty is rarer now in an era of short-term contracts and periodic downsizing.

That said, there are still some remarkable orthodoxies of thought that are common to just about any corporate you can name, not least in the area of creativity. The chains that bind the modern worker are not as obvious as they were in the heyday of nineteenth-century industrialism and now they tend to be self-applied, whether through ignorance or unthinking acceptance of company methods and manners. They may not be drugging the water cooler, but hanging around it long enough may do much the same for you if you absorb the received approach to work and idea generation.

For example, there can be nothing more important for keeping yourself and your business fresh than new ideas. The vast majority of companies, however, rely on creative 'brainstorming' as their principal route to new ideas. Effective brainstorming takes good organisation of time (relax and reflection periods and excited rapid-fire interaction), mutual respect within the group (everyone free to express their ideas and open to others), and a sophisticated synthesis phase where raw ideas are converted to practical application. Funny how often that translates to a roomful of bored people with two loud-mouths running their own show.

HERE'S AN IDEA FOR YOU...

Try a SCAMPER checklist:

Substitute – what can we swap?

Combine – what new things can be brought together?

Adapt – how can we alter the existing?

Modify – what can we change?

Put to another use – reinvention

Eliminate – if we take this out, does it still work?

Reverse – turn it around – does it work better?

16 MULTI SKILL

'In consequence of thus finding out that I am fit to any sort of work, I feel less of a mollusc and more of a man.' This miraculous sprouting of spine does not actually come from Marx but *'...a French workman, on his return from San Francisco'*. Marx is impressed enough by the Frenchman's leap from snail to sapiens to dwell on it at length and in the process give us all a steer about how to live life.

Marx goes on to explain that this Mollusc to Man metamorphosis was brought about by simply turning the hand to a number of trades rather than being pigeon-holed in one. He quotes the French workman as saying that 'I never could have believed, that I was capable of working at the various occupations I was employed on in California. I was firmly convinced that I was fit for nothing but letter-press printing…Once in the midst of this world of adventurers, who change their occupation as often as they do their shirt, egad, I did as the others. As mining did not turn out remunerative enough, I left it for the town, where in succession I became typographer, slater, plumber, etc.'

I'm unsure how many adventurers, slaters, plumbers, etc. wander around using the word 'egad' these days, or even in those days, but Molluscman's epiphany is definitely just as relevant to Modern Man. Changing your occupation as often as you change your shirt is a pretty tall order, but changing your mindset to consider new and often very different options is a great way of bringing a new dimension to your working life and broadening your career.

There's a classic trap in working life which is to end up doing something because you are good at it, not because you happen to like it. In many industries it is entirely normal for someone to start on a hands-on aspect of the work only to be promoted into management and be taken away from any direct input at all. This may work just fine for most, but for some it was the hands-on approach that attracted them in the first place. Similarly, a lot of management works by rewarding people with enough money so that they stop asking themselves whether they enjoy their job. Ask an eight year old what they want to be when they grow up and if they answer 'actuary', 'real estate agent' or 'middle manager' then they deserve to have their lunch money stolen. Get to the age of forty, however, and most of us have completely forgotten the idea that work should be something you wanted to do.

Don't forget, you don't have to be good at something for it to be good at you. Maybe you won't ever be the best slater or plumber – but if that makes you happy then you're a better person than the world's best, but most miserable, letter-press printer.

HERE'S AN IDEA FOR YOU…

You don't have to quit tomorrow and join the circus (though good on you if you do). You can retrain or start a new line in your own time, to see how it goes or as balance for the day job. I know many people who began their new departures as part-time hobbies while working a nine to five.

17 KINKY CAPITALISM – THE FETISHISM OF COMMODITIES

'In order, therefore, to find an analogy, we must have recourse to the mist-enveloped regions of the religious world. In that world the productions of the human brain appear as independent beings endowed with life, and entering into relation both with one another and the human race. So it is in the world of commodities with the products of men's hands. This I call the Fetishism which attaches itself to the products of labour, so soon as they are produced as commodities.'

DEFINING IDEA...

Independence – is loyalty to one's best self and principles, and this is often disloyalty to the general idols and fetishes.

~ MARK TWAIN

Commodity fetishism sounds like the sort of thing Conservative politicians get caught doing with ladies they're not married to, but in the Marxist sense it isn't half as much fun as it sounds. The Marxist concept of commodity fetishism is attributing an objective value to a commodity instead of being able to perceive that the real value of any commodity comes from the complex social relations and labour that went into producing it. Because we don't see the social relations that go into commodities, and instead see the market apparently deciding worth and who does what, those commodities, those productions, appear to form, meet and exchange without any human intervention. They assume a sense of importance, even a sense of life, just as a fetish in some primitive societies is seen as being imbued with a sense of power.

In a modern light, consumerism has been taken to a level that Marx could barely have imagined, and the fetishism associated with objects is now commonplace. You could say that the entire advertising industry was geared towards commodity fetishism, with its emphasis on branding and identity to the point where products are no longer seen as simple things but as the means of building your own personal identity. Status, in particular, is seen as being defined by things: symbols with ever more tenuous claims to their suggested nature. The starting point is that clearly the person who drives the luxury car is of higher status than those who actually built it. From there, however, branding goes further to suggest that it is the car itself that carries the status as its gift and it bestows that (temporarily) upon the lucky owner. By tagging the status firmly to the object we simultaneously undermine, even lose, the actual sense of human status. We even take everyday tools – objects that play music or make phone calls – and talk about them as being 'sexy'. The implicit suggestion is that the user is imbued with a heightened degree of sexiness simply by the association of possession. Which, come to think about it, does rather bring us back to the domain of politicians' peccadillos.

Marx would probably be baffled by modern branding with its complex series of associations and identities tacked onto inanimate objects. On the other hand, he would certainly have seen his theory of commodity fetishism illustrated beyond any doubt whatsoever.

HERE'S AN IDEA FOR YOU...

Are you guilty of judging other individuals and organisations by the associations of objects? Be sure to ask yourself if the status symbol is in recognition of achievement, or if the sense of status is being borrowed from the object. Be sure you're judging the person, not the juju.

18 FORGET THE MORAL MAJORITY

'Temperate living and constant employment is the direct road, for the poor, to rational happiness,' says de Mandeville in the Fable of the Bees, to which Marx retorts '...*by which he most probably means long working-days and little means of subsistence*'. He may have been writing in the era of Victorian values but the bearded wonder never fell for the line that clean living and honest toil were their own reward.

DEFINING IDEA...

The harder a man works, at brute labour, the thinner becomes his idealism, the darker his mind.

– D.H. LAWRENCE

Bernard de Mandeville's Fable of the Bees caused much speculation when it appeared but most of that was about whether it was a subtle dig at the church. In the main, however, the poem describes a prosperous beehive (usually taken to mean England) which is purged of fraud by God and finds subsequent life immensely hard but ultimately happy and its own reward. In the end the newly purged bees are so hardened with toil that '...they counted Ease it self a Vice', which can be seen to fit with his assertion that 'it is the interest of all rich nations, that the greatest part of the poor should almost never be idle, and yet continually spend what they get'. Marx agreed that the richness of a nation was formed by keeping the proletariat working flat out just to keep going, but he was clearly unimpressed with the assertion that hard work is its own reward. Maybe he was just sick of hearing it coming from the mouths of prosperous Victorians exhorting their badly paid workforces to make them more money.

In any case, it is refreshing to see that Marx never once suggested that the way to improvement was just to work harder. Instead he wanted to open the eyes of workers to the fact that their work was being appropriated by an owning class who reaped the benefits while preaching to them about the moral benefits of their self-sacrifice.

Few of us work in sweatshops these days, but a great many of us continue to labour (in both senses) under the weight of a moral judgement about work – that it is somehow a reward in itself. This moralistic, even religious, idea of work as innately rewarding was noted by both Marx and his co-contributor Friedrich Engels. In his synopsis of *Das Kapital*, Engels even points out that 'for a society in which commodity production prevails, Christianity, particularly Protestantism, is the fitting religion'.

Well, don't buy it. Working hard is not in itself bad, but nor is it good – particularly if it is part of an ethos where working hard is seen as somehow better than working smart.

To really contribute to your business or yourself you should reject the orthodoxy of being seen to work hard and instead look for the 'juice' – the essential elements that really matter when it comes to reaching goals. Working on anything else is delusion or diversion.

HERE'S AN IDEA FOR YOU...

Try the Pareto principle approach – that 80% of results come from 20% of time or effort. Similarly 80% of efforts only produce 20% of the results, meaning we're all wasting a lot of time. Write a ten – point list of your to-dos and rank them 1–10 in descending importance. Now forget about points three to ten until one and two are done.

19 COULD TRY HARDER – READING THE REPORTS

Marx draws some of his most damning conclusions from official reports, for example the labour reports that provide
'…documentary evidence of the constant lowering of the price of labour from the beginning of the anti-Jacobin War. In the weaving industry, e.g., piece-wages had fallen so low that, in spite of the very great lengthening of the working-day, the daily wages were then lower than before.'

DEFINING IDEA…

Evil report carries further than any applause.

– BALTASAR GRACIAN,
SPANISH PHILOSOPHER

Reporting may seem dull, but Marx proves that it can be the first step to revolution. Much of the weight of his argument comes not from his somewhat convoluted and repetitive theories about use value and capital, but from his observations about the condition of the working man from the industrial revolution up to Victorian times. Where possible that information came first hand, but he also took the time to extensively study the official documentation of the day to get a glimpse of the bigger picture. Then, as now, records turned out to be the key not only to the past but also to creating a better future.

Sustainable capitalism in all its forms (environmental, social, ethical et al.) is only truly sustainable if it is seen to be sustainable and when a company's commitment to it can be demonstrated. Fortunately, transparency is one of the underlying concepts of the whole approach which should make it all easy – but a lot of organisations don't really take that aspect to heart for one of two reasons. Either they have got sidetracked by the touchy-feely sound of social responsibility and failed to treat it with the rigour they would apply to 'normal' business, or they are quietly indulging in a spot of greenwashing.

Greenwashing is the art of window-dressing business so it has the appearance of social responsibility while in reality carrying on with cold-hearted capitalism behind the scenes. Classic examples of greenwashing include all of those hotels you've stayed in that have a sign in the bathroom asking you to re-use your towels to help save the environment. If that was really the hotel's principal concern (rather than cost-cutting) then they would also have extensive recycling systems, energy saving light bulbs and community projects. Some probably do. Most don't. Good reporting would make that clear instantly.

Other classics of the unsubstantiated include vague claims such as 'natural', 'environment-friendly' or 'healthy', and the principle of diverting attention from the real problems such as labelling products 'CFC free' (CFCs have been banned for two decades) or 'energy efficient' (while neglecting to mention that the energy efficient process involves toxic chemicals.

Even such seemingly bullet proof guarantees as 'certified organic' mean nothing if the certification can't be verified. In 2007 an organic marketing company called TerraChoice surveyed 1100 household products and found that over 450 of them made claims along those lines that could not be checked.

Reporting and documentation are essential to a responsible approach to capitalism – without it any exercise in social responsibility is little more than lip service, no matter how earnestly it starts out.

HERE'S AN IDEA FOR YOU...

Starting out with reporting on sustainability is a daunting task, so take a leaf from the experts and look at the Global Reporting Initiative (GRI): Sustainability Reporting Guidelines for some ideas. The GRI guidelines are available from www.globalreporting.org.

20 CRISIS, WHAT CRISIS?

'Industrial revulsions affect even the best paid, the aristocracy, of the working-class. It will be remembered that the year 1857 brought one of the great crises with which the industrial cycle periodically ends. The next termination of the cycle was due in 1866.' **Marx saw crisis as part of the regular cycle of industry – we might do well to look at the current downturn in the same light.**

At time of writing (early '09) the media is consumed by an orgy of wailing. The woes of the world are all financial and the four horsemen of the apocalypse have turned out to be a bunch of bankers on BMWs.

Without wanting to belittle the misery of those suffering hardship, the language of the media would suggest that what we're experiencing is the end of the world, rather than a correction of some wildly irresponsible financial markets. Even the news that BP has shown a 39% annual rise in profits (39%!) is announced in gloomy terms because its chief executive may be leaving (as if nobody else would be willing to step into his shoes). Marx would not have been surprised. He noted that the financial markets appear to have the kind of short-term memory that would make them a laughing stock amongst goldfish. Writing of the cotton industry he embarks on a whirlwind tour of its fortunes during the heyday of British industry.

'From 1815 to 1821 depression; 1822 and 1823 prosperity; 1824 abolition of the laws against Trades' Unions, great extension of factories everywhere; 1825 crisis; 1826 great misery and riots among the factory operatives; 1827 slight improvement; 1828 great increase in power-looms, and in exports; 1829 exports, especially to India, surpass all former years; 1830 glutted markets, great distress; 1831 to 1833 continued depression, …1836 great prosperity; 1837 and 1838 depression and crisis; 1839 revival; 1840 great depression, riots, calling out of the military…1844 revival; 1845 great prosperity; 1846 continued improvement at first, then reaction. Repeal of the Corn Laws; 1847 crisis…1854 prosperity, glutted markets; 1855 news of failures stream in from the United States, Canada, and the Eastern markets; 1856 great prosperity; 1857 crisis; 1858 improvement; 1859 great prosperity, increase in factories; 1860 Zenith of the English cotton trade…1861 prosperity continues for a time, reaction, the American Civil War, cotton famine: 1862 to 1863 complete collapse.'

1866 saw the great collapse of the money market: 'the crisis assumed, at this time, an especially financial character. Its outbreak in 1866 was signalised by the failure of a gigantic London Bank, immediately followed by the collapse of countless swindling companies.'

Sounds familiar? Marx makes the point that boom and bust is the characteristic of the system which works to constantly expand, driving demand and periodically oversupplying it. The current crisis may be the worst for some time, but fewer people are likely to starve in the streets as a result and it will pass (until the next one).

HERE'S AN IDEA FOR YOU…

When you go skiing you take out insurance because it's risky. Why not protect your livelihood? A monthly policy will usually insure around 60% of your income. Mortgage protection policies secure your home. Just be aware that most won't pay if you're self-employed or your business is already announcing job cuts.

21 ON A NEURAL PATHWAY TO HELL

'At the same time that factory work exhausts the nervous system to the uttermost, it does away with the many-sided play of the muscles, and confiscates every atom of freedom, both in bodily and intellectual activity.'

DEFINING IDEA...

Inventive genius requires pleasurable mental activity as a condition for its vigorous exercise.

– ALFRED NORTH WHITEHEAD, BRITISH MATHEMATICIAN AND PHILOSOPHER

Not only does all work and no play make Jack a dull boy, but specifically doing the same thing over and over makes him stupid. Marx was way ahead of his time in saying this, and the importance of the learning experience in ensuring mental agility has since been so well established that it has actually become an industry in its own right. Studies into the roles of neural pathways have shown that challenging your brain to learn new skills and ways of thinking – such as learning a new language, a musical instrument or a sport – helps make connections in the brain. The brain, it seems, is a work in progress and if you continually do new things it will continue to form new connections and links, becoming fitter, much like a muscle. In effect, you either use it or lose it. Studies in Japan suggest that just 15 minutes of puzzling your grey cells every day can help keep those synapses and may even slow the effects of ageing. A whole industry has sprung up to promote brain teasers and computer learning games that promise to keep your grey cells on their toes. One, Nintendo's Dr Kawashima's Brain Training: How Old is Your Brain?, became a national bestseller and is now widely sold in other markets.

So not only do we become extraordinarily dull if we only live and breathe our jobs (insert your favourite accountant joke here) but we may actually be dulling our wits in the process. The problem is that dull jobs often bring with them a sense of routine and routine has its own invisible shackles that are every bit as constricting as the repressive work practices of Victorian industry. How many times do we talk of someone getting stuck in a rut? Of course, it's easier to say that about someone else than to admit it about ourselves but think carefully about your own role – when was the last time you left your comfort zone and were challenged by something new at work? Today? Yesterday? Last week? Last year? If you aren't regularly having to apply your mind to new challenges then you may literally be losing the ability to do so. Oh, and your small talk will be pants.

We often look down on people who constantly take up new fads and then let them drop, but it seems that may be better for them than not taking up any new interests at all. We all have at least one friend who is forever announcing a new love in life (to the accompaniment of much rolling of eyeballs from the rest of us) but their puppyish enthusiasm for all things new may actually be helping to hold off the ageing process.

HERE'S AN IDEA FOR YOU...

You don't have to become fluent in Mandarin or learn to fly a helicopter to stretch your brain. Varying your mental routine with puzzles such as crosswords and Sudoku or even listening to new music can also stimulate your brain (although becoming a Mandarin-speaking helicopter pilot might open new career paths).

22 FIT FOR PURPOSE?

'The collective labourer now possesses, in an equal degree of excellence, all the qualities requisite for production, and expends them in the most economical manner, by exclusively employing all his organs, consisting of particular labourers, or groups of labourers, in performing their special functions.'

That sounds rather good, doesn't it? 'Qualities requisite', 'economical manner', 'employing all his organs', 'performing their special functions' – all of that makes the collective labourer sound like a bit of a superman. That's it – I'm not an office drone, I'm Spidey.

DEFINING IDEA...

Physical fitness is not only one of the most important keys to a healthy body, it is the basis of dynamic and creative intellectual activity.

~ JOHN F. KENNEDY

Except that, if you read on, Karl adds a slightly worrying clarification: 'The one-sidedness and the deficiencies of the detail labourer become perfections when he is a part of the collective labourer.' Since when did 'one-sidedness' and 'deficiency' become perfections? The answer is when you are no longer considering the worker as a human being, and are instead only concerned with his function as an adjunct to the machine. Any doubt that this is what Marx is saying can be dispelled by reference to the footnote that accompanies his idea of 'deficiency' – 'For instance, abnormal development of some muscles, curvature of bones, etc.' Meaning that even if you have been literally bent out of shape by the job it means you're probably better equipped to serve the purpose of the system.

Which is all well and good for the system, but not so hot for those of us who like to maintain the illusion that we're individuals. Not to mention individuals that occasionally have to walk past full-length mirrors.

Physical fitness has been shown to be an invaluable weapon in the worker's armoury, and not least because it helps to counter stress. Increased cardiovascular capacity works to reduce stress-related conditions, such as tension and high blood pressure, and by helping to keep weight to a sensible limit, fitness can also help reduce factors like body fat that can further exacerbate stress-related diseases. Getting in shape personally is a better way to get in shape professionally, and since it boosts your self-esteem it's more likely to make you feel like a winner and less like a twisted piece of a bigger machine.

You don't have to go to the gym to get the benefit of improved fitness – walking is excellent exercise and an easy one to build into your working (walking?) day. Walk to the train station, get off the bus a stop early and walk the last leg to the office, walk up stairs rather than take the lift or use an escalator, walk over to see a colleague rather than sending them an email. Buy a bicycle, use it to go to the shops (buy a lock, too, if you want it to still be there for your return journey), make a pact with a colleague to go running (or walking, or jogging), dust off that old tennis/squash racket and make your long overdue reappearance on the sports court.

HERE'S AN IDEA FOR YOU...

Nobody looking? Great, try modified press-ups at your desk. Stand four feet from your desk, feet together, hands on the desk top and shoulder-width apart. Keep your back nice and straight and slowly bend your elbows so your chest dips to the desk. Try five to ten repetitions twice a day.

23 SHINE ON

'But in its blind unrestrainable passion, its were-wolf hunger for surplus-labour, capital oversteps not only the moral, but even the merely physical maximum bounds of the working-day. It usurps the time for growth, development, and healthy maintenance of the body. It steals the time required for the consumption of fresh air and sunlight.'

DEFINING IDEA...

There is no investment you can make which will pay you so well as the effort to scatter sunshine and good cheer through your establishment.

– ORISON SWETT MARDEN.
WRITER AND PHILOSOPHER

Marx noted that fresh air and sunlight are essential to a healthy happy life and backed up his point with medical authority. 'On the importance of sunlight for the maintenance and growth of the body, a physician writes: "Light also acts upon the tissues of the body directly in hardening them and supporting their elasticity. The muscles of animals, when they are deprived of a proper amount of light, become soft and inelastic, the nervous power loses its tone from defective stimulation, and the elaboration of all growth seems to be perverted…"'

We don't have to get to the point where growth is perverted to be suffering from a lack of sunlight and fresh air – it usually just affects us in terms of mood. We all know how opening the curtains to face a bright sunny day helps lighten our mood, and it's no accident that the happiest amongst us are said to have a 'sunny' disposition. It wasn't realised for a long time that bright light wasn't just a luxury option in life – a shortage of it can trigger serious depression in the form of seasonal affective disorder (SAD). SAD symptoms typically kick in around October/November (in the northern hemisphere) and fade away in spring. Symptoms include listlessness, depression and lack of enthusiasm. The closer to the pole you live, the worse it's likely to be. The obvious answer, if your lifestyle can allow it, is to turn into a 'swallow' and simply swap the northern hemisphere for the southern as autumn sets in, thereby ensuring continuous spring/summer. It's a nice idea, but it's not for everybody – so if you think that the lack of light is getting you down, you're going to have to take some less drastic steps to lighting up your life.

One of the key things is that unless you live in the Arctic Circle then you probably do get light in winter – it's just that you're not exposing yourself to enough of it. Getting up before dawn to go to work is enough to get anybody down, and finding that it's dark when you go home from work is enough to paint a truly dark picture. Yet how few of us go out of our way to deliberately get out of the office and into the daylight during the day? In winter there is all the more reason to get outside – tell everyone to grab their coats and hold that meeting outdoors clutching steaming mugs of coffee. Take the time to go out for lunch even if it means eating sandwiches while walking in the park.

HERE'S AN IDEA FOR YOU...

Bright light treatment dramatically reduces SAD. It was thought that expensive 'full spectrum' bulbs were required, but these days relatively cheap lamps are enclosed in a light box with a diffusing lens to protect you from ultraviolet radiation. Exposure to the box, even for 20 minutes or so a day, can help – so try a floodlit breakfast.

24 IDOLATRY

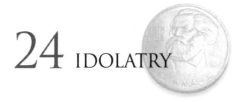

'And modern economy, which looks down with such disdain on the monetary system, does not its superstition come out as clear as noon-day, whenever it treats of capital?'

DEFINING IDEA...

Superstition, idolatry, and hypocrisy have ample wages, but truth goes a-begging.

~ MARTIN LUTHER

Considering that Marx once famously dismissed religion as 'the opium of the people' it's interesting to see that his own criticism of the modern economy was recently picked up on and elaborated by none other than Rowan Williams, the Archbishop of Canterbury. He complained that not only does the financial world need serious scrutiny and rigorous regulation, but that our attitude to it to date smacks of idolatry.

'Fundamentalism', begins the Archbishop, 'is a religious word, not inappropriate to the nature of the problem. Marx long ago observed the way in which unbridled capitalism became a kind of mythology, ascribing reality, power and agency to things that had no life in themselves; he was right about that, if about little else.'

Leaving aside whether or not Marx was indeed 'right about little else', what's interesting here is that religion and Marxism have fallen into step about the attitude of society to modern economy. The successive influences of Thatcher, Reagan and Bush have combined to create an orthodoxy that the market is the ultimate decider and market forces, preferably market forces entirely unhindered by government interference, can and should shape economies and the fate of nations. As Archbishop Williams puts it: 'We find ourselves talking about capital or the market almost as if they were individuals, with purposes and strategies, making choices, deliberating reasonably about how to achieve aims. We lose sight of the fact that they are things that we make.'

Not only do we act as if markets arose independently of human action, but we also assume that with their functioning comes a sort of built-in consciousness: 'We expect an abstraction called "the market" to produce the common good or to regulate its potential excesses by a sort of natural innate prudence, like a physical organism or ecosystem.'

The credit crunch of 2009 did not signal the failure of the free-market economy, any more than the fall of the Berlin Wall and the break up of the Soviet Union signalled the end of Marxism (Marx would have struggled to recognise his beliefs in their Soviet implementation). What it should do, however, is serve as a reminder that such systems are deeply flawed and not above criticism. Anyone who still believes that market forces alone should operate untrammelled should be shipped off to Iceland to explain that to a population currently debating not whether to oust its government (they've already done that) but whether to do away with its entire political class.

'The mythologies and abstractions, the pseudo-objects of much modern financial culture, are in urgent need of their own Dawkins or Hitchens,' says Archbishop Williams – interestingly calling for market equivalents of these famous atheists. What the Bish seems to have missed is that capitalism already has its Dawkins – a man called Marx.

HERE'S AN IDEA FOR YOU...

Non-executive board members don't have to cost more than a few lunches and are a great way to get a conflicting but complementary view. Think laterally. Running an out-and-out creative company? Get an unreconstructed manufacturer as a non-executive director. In accountancy? Get a flamboyant creative on the board.

25 PUTTING WORDS INTO THE MOUTHS OF OTHERS

Railing against the harm caused by industrialisation Marx declared that *'Whoever, therefore, exposes the real state of things in the capitalistic employment of machinery, is against its employment in any way, and is an enemy of social progress! Exactly the reasoning of the celebrated Bill Sykes.'*

DEFINING IDEA...

Facts are ventriloquist's dummies.

~ ALDOUS HUXLEY

Karl goes on to expound Sykes' rationale, quoting the Dickensian ruffian as saying 'Gentlemen of the jury, no doubt the throat of this commercial traveller has been cut. But that is not my fault, it is the fault of the knife. Must we, for such a temporary inconvenience, abolish the use of the knife? Only consider! where would agriculture and trade be without the knife? Is it not as salutary in surgery, as it is knowing in anatomy? And in addition a willing help at the festive board? If you abolish the knife – you hurl us back into the depths of barbarism.'

A fine argument, and compellingly made. In order to expose the imagined criticism of his own reasoning, Marx borrows the self-justifications of a cut-throat and suggests that this absurd argument is in fact that of his critics.

Similarly, when discussing the use of child labour, Marx promptly personifies capital by making it into a person and giving it a voice. In this case the voice is of Shylock from Shakespeare's Merchant of Venice: 'Workmen and factory inspectors protested on hygienic and moral grounds, but Capital answered: "My deeds upon my head! I crave the law, The penalty and forfeit of my bond."'

As it happens Bill Sykes never said anything of the kind. Marx has skilfully pulled a double whammy by not only borrowing a fictional character to stand in for his critics, but conveniently making up that character's speech. He has, in fact, not only put words into the mouths of his critics but done so by putting words into the mouth of a made-up spokesman. Sly old beardy.

I wouldn't be the first to suggest that this could well imply a sense of tongue-in-cheek roguishness. This is, after all, the same man who protested that he himself was not Marxist, and who is commonly and unfairly judged in the light of the dour and despotic regimes who claimed to have been inspired by him. Personally I suspect that the bushy facial fungus may well have served to hide a little cheeky grin from time to time, and his invention of Sykes' speech is a good example.

The lesson to learn is that dry ideas come to life and resonate much more forcibly when put into the mouth of a character. Instead of running through points of view on paper, or minute by minute in a meeting, try assigning each one to an individual and have them debated that way. If you have an argument to make, encourage your audience to imagine the words coming from the mouths of a key rival or role model, as appropriate.

HERE'S AN IDEA FOR YOU...

Hire a licensed fool. Microsoft's marketing division, aware that the company was unpopular but not wanting to spell out why themselves, used to bring journalists in to address senior management and tell them why they were hated. The journalists said nothing marketing didn't know, but senior staff listened and there was no internal awkwardness afterwards.

26 PICK YOUR FIGHTS CAREFULLY

'Classical economy always loved to conceive social capital as a fixed magnitude of a fixed degree of efficiency. But this prejudice was first established as a dogma by the arch-Philistine, Jeremy Bentham, that insipid, pedantic, leather-tongued oracle of the ordinary bourgeois intelligence of the 19th century.'

DEFINING IDEA...

In a fight between you and the world, pick the world.

~ FRANK ZAPPA

Whoa – rewind there a little, Karl…Maybe that was just a little creative outburst, a little spark of spite in the flow of reason. Entirely forgiveable, except that like a dog with a bone, or a drunk with a half-baked argument, old Karl just won't let it go. He has to go and add a footnote: 'Bentham is a purely English phenomenon. Not even excepting our philosopher, Christian Wolff, in no time and in no country has the most homespun commonplace ever strutted about in so self-satisfied a way.'

Heavens Karl, what did this guy do? 'With the driest naiveté he takes the modern shopkeeper, especially the English shopkeeper, as the normal man.' The horror, the horror.

'Bentham', Marx goes on, 'is among philosophers what Martin Tupper is among poets. Both could only have been manufactured in England.' Most of us are wondering where Tupper came from, but to Karl he and Bentham are clearly interlinked since he accuses Bentham of saying that 'Artistic criticism is "harmful," because it disturbs worthy people in their enjoyment of Martin Tupper, etc. With such rubbish has the brave fellow, with his motto, "nuila dies sine line!," piled up mountains of books. Had I the courage of my friend, Heinrich Heine, I should call Mr. Jeremy a genius in the way of bourgeois stupidity.'

Seems to me, Karl, that you just did.

Time hasn't been kind to Karl here, since Jeremy Bentham is largely remembered as a liberal moderniser and Tupper, if he can be said to be remembered at all, is known as a dabbler in poetry and an early fan of African Literature. There's no getting away from the fact that Karl is tilting at windmills here. The reader doesn't care about Bentham or his shopkeepers, and Tupper is entirely irrelevant, so why does Marx get his knickers in such a twist about them?

What we're seeing is the fact that even in the densely packed economic workings of Das Kapital there is a purely personal irritability showing through. It really stands out because Marx hasn't even disguised it well. It's not isolated either; he dismisses MacCulloch as 'a past master in this pretentious cretinism'; says of Ganilh: 'It is not possible to bring out the cretinism of his standpoint' and Russia earns '…the applause of liberal cretins throughout Europe.' Marx is positively spitting blood but he doesn't even have the sense to dress his windmills up as legitimate targets. If he really wanted to have a go at Tupper, he could have dug up the allegations that the poet declared 'The world is a world for the Anglo Saxon race!' which might have merited a footnote.

HERE'S AN IDEA FOR YOU...

Never go into a fight without thinking what positive result you want from it. Literally pick your fights – draw up a list of what's at stake, the likelihood of success and what you need to do to win. If you're not clear about these then don't go in swinging – in fact, don't go in at all.

27 LOOK AT YOUR HUMAN CREDIT TERMS

'The purchase of labour-power for a fixed period is the prelude to the process of production; and this prelude is constantly repeated when the stipulated term comes to an end, when a definite period of production, such as a week or a month, has elapsed.'

DEFINING IDEA...

Loss-making businesses can survive, but businesses that run out of cash will not.

– MICHAEL IZZA, CHIEF EXECUTIVE, INSTITUTE OF CHARTERED ACCOUNTANTS IN ENGLAND AND WALES, IN 2008

Marx spends a great deal of *Das Kapital* analysing the principles behind the working day and the wage set for it. One of the key points he makes is that while labour is sold in periods (usually a day, a week or a month) the capitalist never pays up front so the transaction is always skewed towards the provider of work. 'But the labourer is not paid until after he has expended his labour-power, and realised in commodities not only its value, but surplus-value. He has, therefore, produced not only surplus-value, which we for the present regard as a fund to meet the private consumption of the capitalist, but he has also produced, before it flows back to him in the shape of wages, the fund out of which he himself is paid, the variable capital; and his employment lasts only so long as he continues to reproduce this fund.'

What that means is that the worker is effectively lending his labour to the capitalist, interest free, and is only ever paid in arrears. Which seems pretty unfair when you think about it – after all, it tends to be the case that the capitalist, rather than the labourer, is the one who least needs the loan. Most of us are paid monthly, but we do the full month's work before we get paid for it. Jobs where you are paid in advance are as rare as hen's teeth, and are usually either highly risky, highly illegal or both.

Nor is all this about to change overnight; after all, this skewed system of lending labour to the capitalist has come about because the job provider has the whip hand in the majority of employment. What's more, that is never more true than in an economic downturn when work is scarcer and the employer's position is strengthened further. However, it is possible to take a look at the system and use it more efficiently.

Most businesses, and pretty much all self-employed people, will appreciate the idea of cash flow in advance since maintaining positive cash flow can even be more important than generating profit in some situations. So take a look at your suppliers, or your client list if you are on the supplier side, and see if there's a case anywhere for switching from periodic invoicing to a smaller sum but paid out in regular increments during the process – effectively switching from paying monthly to paying weekly but negotiating a different rate in the process. Don't forget that half now, half later doesn't just have to be for hit men; it can prove surprisingly attractive to all sorts of businesses.

HERE'S AN IDEA FOR YOU...

Structure your pricing scale so you reward early payment with discounts – a sliding scale where payment goes up the later it gets is not difficult to thrash out and agree on, and liquidity may well be more important to you or your business than trading your goods or services for the highest price.

28 FOR HEAVEN'S SAKE, CHEER UP

'Accumulation of wealth at one pole is, therefore, at the same time accumulation of misery, agony of toil, slavery, ignorance, brutality, mental degradation, at the opposite pole, i.e., on the side of the class that produces its own product in the form of capital.'

DEFINING IDEA...

One day I sat thinking… 'Cheer up, things could be worse.' So I cheered up, and sure enough, things got worse.
– JAMES C. HAGERTY,
WHITE HOUSE PRESS SECRETARY

I'm sure Karl was a barrel of laughs when he relaxed over a pint down the pub but reading *Das Kapital* makes it clear that his observations of nineteenth-century industry had left him with an unremittingly bleak impression of working life. He felt that where once work had an innate appeal for the worker, it had been broken down by the increasing sophistication of piece-work and the assembly line to the point where it was at best monotonous and at worst a soul-destroying process destined to grind the worker down. 'They [the capitalists] mutilate the labourer into a fragment of a man, degrade him to the level of an appendage of a machine, destroy every remnant of charm in his work and turn it into a hated toil.'

Unless you're in a particularly bad place in life, the chances are that you haven't really done a job you could class as 'hated toil' since your very early years when you took on short-term work to make a bit of extra money when you weren't studying. Now, if you're in management, you're probably in a position where you can make a difference to the hated toil of others. So take the time to make that difference. What Marx failed to foresee was the advent of 'caring capitalism' in which the more huggy businesses go out of their way to make their staff happier. Ben and Jerry, the ice cream makers, established a reputation for treating their staff well to increase worker happiness. That may have sprung in part from their hippy backgrounds but there is a more hard-nosed side to it, too, in terms of issues like staff retention and reducing absenteeism. They introduced a novel approach to lightening toil by appointing people whose job it is to stop the daily grind from actually being a grind. Those people are called The Joy Gang. They are all volunteers and are in charge of an annual budget which they assign to different activities that they agree will make the most difference to the day to day routine. That has taken the form of massage at work, free pizza days, dress badly days, and, rather disturbingly, a Barry Manilow appreciation day.

Joy Gang sounds like the sort of euphemism that a communist dictatorship might come up with, but the idea behind it – of putting worker happiness on the agenda as a topic to be discussed and invested in – is one that can be applied to any line of business. It doesn't have to be expensive, just sincerely applied. With so much economic doom and gloom being discussed it would do everyone a favour to look on the bright side.

HERE'S AN IDEA FOR YOU...

Start your own cheerfulness committee. Let volunteers be voted on by staff and make it their job to come up with suggestions for improving the happiness of all. Have them not only cost each suggestion, but also come up with metrics to judge their success – like improved timekeeping or a 'happiness meter' of their choice.

29 BE SPECIAL

'In order to modify the human organism, so that it may acquire skill and handiness in a given branch of industry, and become labour-power of a special kind, a special education or training is requisite, and this, on its part, costs an equivalent in commodities of a greater or less amount.'

Marx may have been a great believer in collectivism but he recognised that actually not all workers are equal and that some, thanks to their 'skill and handiness', can be considered as 'labour-power of a special kind'.

DEFINING IDEA...

Man is an animal that makes bargains: no other animal does this – no dog exchanges bones with another.

– ADAM SMITH

Within the factory system he saw that possibility as limited and he quotes at length the 1854 committee report of The Master Spinners' and Manufacturers' Defence Fund which says that: 'The factory operatives should keep in wholesome remembrance the fact that theirs is really a low species of skilled labour; and that there is none which is more easily acquired, or of its quality more amply remunerated, or which by a short training of the least expert can be more quickly, as well as abundantly, acquired.'

In short, the workers are nothing but foot soldiers and cannon fodder. That, however, is not true of the modern workplace since it is clear that by acquiring skills the foot soldier can rise up the ranks, and while it might be a bit naïve to say the sky's the limit, it is certainly true that with a bit of self-improvement you can make more of yourself – or at least demand better pay for the work that you are doing.

Of course work isn't just about the money. It's about the comradeship, the sense of spiritual enrichment and the opportunity to pilfer stationery and goof about on company time. Somehow, though, salary does keep on coming up and the chances are that it's a big part of why you bother to turn up on Monday morning. So don't pretend you wouldn't like a little extra.

If you want to be special you'll need to start asking what it is that you do well, what you feel the job (or job market) most wants that you have and what you could do better. Start off by asking yourself the following questions:

1. How would my colleagues describe me, professionally?

2. What are my best attributes?

3. What is my target market – my current boss, a potential new employer?

4. What have I done recently to raise my profile with that target market?

5. What do I plan on doing to raise my profile with my target market?

What you do next depends on your answers to questions number one to four, but options include seeking out further training/certification, proposing your own projects or even approaching the trade press for your business with a view to penning an opinion piece or being profiled. Whatever you choose to do, be sure that you are doing it with a view to reaching your target market, not just flattering your ego.

HERE'S AN IDEA FOR YOU...

Want to know what you might be worth? Don't just compare with your immediate colleagues (presuming you're prepared to share salary information) as that just gives you the picture within one company and industry. Instead try an online salary checker; they're available for pretty much every industry and part of the world, so why keep yourself in the dark?

30 TRAINING – THE FAST TRACK

'One step already spontaneously taken towards effecting this revolution is the establishment of technical and agricultural schools, and of "écoles d'enseignement professionnel" in which the children of the working-men receive some little instruction in technology and in the practical handling of the various implements of labour.'

DEFINING IDEA...

I always say we don't have a worker shortage in this country, we have a skill shortage.

– ALEXIS HERMAN, US SECRETARY OF LABOR

Marx felt that the education on offer for the working man was woefully inadequate and very begrudgingly given. He felt sure that, come the revolution, we would see technical skills being taught in the classroom. 'The Factory Act, that first and meagre concession wrung from capital, is limited to combining elementary education with work in the factory, there can be no doubt that when the working-class comes into power, as inevitably it must, technical instruction, both theoretical and practical, will take its proper place in the working-class schools.'

OK, so he may have been a little wrong about the working class inevitably coming into power, since the landed and moneyed classes generally not only seem to have done a good job of holding on to the reins worldwide but are also showing no sign of giving them up any time now. That doesn't mean he was wrong, however, about the importance of 'technical instruction': real-world vocational skills.

The argument rages about the conflicting benefits of a traditional education versus vocational training, but by the time it comes to the workplace we rarely see companies prepared to pay to improve someone's ability in art and literature, while making a good case can often result in a training course in job-related skills. Or at least it should. The problem is that all too often companies presume that there's an unlimited pool of human resources out there and that none of their employees is irreplaceable. That idea usually persists until one of the 'replaceables' ups and leaves.

Training is typically underfunded and often tops the list when companies are looking to make cuts and short-term savings. Which is short-termist in the extreme. A good training system raises morale and improves staff retention. A successful in-house training system is brilliant for creating a company culture which then shows in terms of distinguishing that brand in the market. Any and every company should be an academy of itself – even a one-man band.

If you don't have the resources for formal in-house training, then consider getting a third party in but beware of accepting off-the-shelf solutions if they don't truly apply to the complexities of your business. Either find a specialist company/trainer or have a training company deliver a bespoke curriculum to you – this doesn't have to be expensive if the company believes that success will mean repeat business.

Training isn't just a sensible human investment, it is also a bargaining chip in industrial relations, a huge morale booster, and can be used to groom talent while giving value back to a local community through internships and apprenticeships.

HERE'S AN IDEA FOR YOU...

Job shadowing is a great way to train up the less experienced and share the skills of your experts. Done well, it's also a case of everybody winning since ideally the person sharing should find their own workload eased by the person who is increasing their value by learning.

31 PETTY PERHAPS, BUT NO SMALL DEAL

'The private property of the labourer in his means of production is the foundation of petty industry, whether agricultural, manufacturing, or both; petty industry, again, is an essential condition for the development of social production and of the free individuality of the labourer himself.'

DEFINING IDEA...

I get so tired listening to one million dollars here, one million dollars there, it's so petty.

~ IMELDA MARCOS

Which makes petty industry sound pretty exciting stuff. Marx goes on to say that '[petty industry] flourishes, it lets loose its whole energy, it attains its adequate classical form, only where the labourer is the private owner of his own means of labour set in action by himself: the peasant of the land which he cultivates, the artisan of the tool which he handles as a virtuoso. This mode of production pre-supposes parcelling of the soil and scattering of the other means of production.'

Petty industry has come on a little since the 1860s and soil doesn't really come into it quite as much. The scattering of the means of production, on the other hand, has come on a treat and we have unprecedented access to ways of making a living. The wonder of the Web and the expansion of the knowledge economy mean that we can trade in experience and analysis, rather than things we have made or grown. Petty industry comes on a plate these days for anyone with the drive and the wits to make their own way. Individuals can simply sign up and start trading in shares or foreign currency online. And creating a shop no longer requires a hefty investment in bricks and mortar –

you can set up shop on eBay and instantly have an international reach at the click of a button. A significant number of people go to car-boot sales to find goods which they can sell on via eBay, and some go to eBay just to buy things which they can then resell.

The beauty of setting up shop on eBay is that you can run your very own business without incurring the overheads of rent or rates and in the process experiment with your own entrepreneurial side or simply supplement your income by buying and selling. It's a great way to turn a hobby into a money spinner. Setting up an eBay shop, rather than simply listing items to sell as an individual, gives you the opportunity to create and develop a brand and build up a loyal clientele who may be from anywhere around the world. Unlike individually listed items, an eBay shop means that if something doesn't sell then you don't have to continually re-list it on offer.

It's not free – you need an Internet connection and you'll still have to store your own goods before sale, as well as think about returns. Charges from eBay include listing fees and final value fees (currently starting at just over 5% of the selling price), plus there's a monthly subscription fee if you want to have your own shop – but the most basic shop costs less than £10, so it's hardly a huge hurdle.

HERE'S AN IDEA FOR YOU...

The tax authorities are increasingly taking an interest in eBay shops, so have a word with your accountant. If you're a sole trader, your sales will count as taxable income. If you're a limited company, you'll have to charge VAT on your auctions. You're not invisible just because you conduct your business from the back bedroom.

32 SHACKLED BY SNACKS

'Every master may put an iron ring round the neck, arms or legs of his slave, by which to know him more easily and to be more certain of him. The last part of this statute provides, that certain poor people may be employed by a place or by persons, who are willing to give them food and drink and to find them work.'

Iron rings around the neck are, by and large, frowned upon in modern business as a means of ensuring worker loyalty. Food, on the other hand, is a powerful force and some companies have caught on to the way that it can be used to shackle a workforce to their desks without being accused of slavery.

DEFINING IDEA...

Food is an important part of a balanced diet.

– FRAN LEBOWITZ,
AMERICAN WRITER

Back in the early 1990s Microsoft wasn't just seen as a mega corporation – it still had a reputation as an edgy, savvy kind of place and was presumed to be the natural home of the sharpest minds. As part of that, Microsoft didn't have anything as mundane or industrial as a factory complex in its home town of Redmond; instead it had a 'campus' set amid landscaped lawns, and patrolled by a smiling benevolent security force known to some as the Microsoft Police. If you've ever seen re-runs of the cult 60s programme The Prisoner you'll have a pretty fair idea of what it was like. The most startling thing about the whole place, however, wasn't the sense of being cocooned from reality; it was the fridges.

Huge chill cabinets, fit to fill the wall of your local 7-11, were stocked to overflowing with tins of drinks. Every kind of exotic juice you could think of was represented, but the real pride of place went to the high-caffeine energy drinks. Programming, you see, has a culture of pulling all-nighters and the fridges held the fuel.

Cut to the noughties, and it's clear that some companies are still pulling the same trick. Go into Google's offices (the Googleplex) and you'll find bowls of fruit, bottled water and energy bars. Food is free and more than one Google staffer has laughingly admitted to piling on the pounds while working for the company. The idea is simple. Food is a relatively cheap way of maintaining morale, but better yet is making it instantly available so people are less likely to leave the building during the day. Instead they are far more likely to eat and snack at their desks, or in meetings or huddled on sofas with colleagues in the informal gathering areas, which means that the distractions of the outside world are kept safely at bay and the company milks the maximum from its staff.

A lot of companies that don't have full kitchen facilities at least try to make breakfast available so that workers are more likely to make it to their desks on time. Try the occasional meeting before hours and throw in breakfast as a bribe.

HERE'S AN IDEA FOR YOU...

You don't even have to have a canteen to please your workers; a simple fruit bowl is a step in the right direction. Offset the cost of a few kilos of Granny Smiths against the time lost to external snack breaks – and if the old adage about an apple a day rings true, you can win your money back in reduced absenteeism.

33 STOP LIVING IN THE PAST

'The position of the English agricultural labourer from 1770 to 1780, with regard to his food and dwelling, as well as to his self-respect, amusements, &c., is an ideal never attained again since that time.'

DEFINING IDEA...

Nostalgia isn't what it used to be.

- TRADITIONAL WISDOM

Given the times he was living in, Marx can be forgiven for his nostalgia for a golden age before modern practices began turning agriculture into an intensive industry. This hankering after a pastoral idyll of yesteryear, however, runs the risk of going further and undermining our sense of achievement in what modernity has brought.

Marx's criticisms of his own age are well-researched, well-founded and well-phrased (unlike a lot of his economic theory) but his assumption that the life of pre-industrial agricultural workers marked some kind of high point in terms of 'self-respect, amusements, etc.' is, at best, a bit blinkered.

The past always looks rosier, but never so much as with a bit of truly selective vision. In Marx's golden rural past there is no consideration of the political freedom of that labourer, his right to express himself, or his access to education and certainly not a mention of the living conditions and social status of the women at the time.

Complex society is quick to idealise simple society but without taking into account that the simple life was often an extraordinarily hidebound one based on unthinking servitude either to others or the requirement to survive.

Societies that have opted to go backwards, such as ones run by hardcore Islamic fundamentalists, would appear to have also retreated from most of the civil liberties that had previously developed in their countries.

Fundamentalism may be an extreme example, but the temptation to live a little in the past or hanker after the 'good old days' is a false refuge in confusing times. The newspaper industry, for instance, is one that is facing a crisis not just of income but of identity. Classified advertising revenues have been all but eaten by online services and the availability of instant news on the web means that the newspaper-reading population is both shrinking and ageing. Some newspapers are realising that their own future may lie in purely electronic versions that continue their traditional core values of good writing, reporting and standard-bearing for a certain political/social outlook. Most, however, are desperately trying anything they can to prop up their paper divisions – including (in France) state subsidies and free subscriptions to people reaching the age of 18. The fact that the paper is in trouble precisely because it fails to appeal to 18 year olds does not appear to be addressed with the same energy.

The day of the newspaper isn't over, but the idea of a return to a golden era when we all felt undressed without a daily paper and a hat is frankly ludicrous, and the industry might be better served by facing up to the future and stepping boldly forwards. Can the same be said of your own business?

HERE'S AN IDEA FOR YOU…

Set up a Skunk works. This was originally from warplane manufacture but has come to mean a group within a company given a lot of independence and the remit to invent the future free from the orthodoxy of company thinking. Start by chairing meetings with 'what if?' scenarios that dare to design a very different future.

34 KNOW WHEN TO STOP

'The thing is proceeding very slowly because no sooner does one set about finally disposing of subjects to which one has devoted years of study than they start revealing new aspects and demand to be thought out further.' (Marx, when working on *Das Kapital*.)

DEFINING IDEA...
Simplicity, simplicity, simplicity! I say...
– HENRY DAVID THOREAU

There's a story about Pixar's 2003 blockbuster Finding Nemo – the animated tale of a heroic quest to reunite a clown fish with his father. In order to pitch the idea to Pixar head honcho John Lasseter, the would-be director, Andrew Stanton, spent over an hour trying to create a sense of the film's atmosphere, feel and characters with a whole cast of characters, voices and visual aids. Lasseter sat through the whole thing and finally a nervous Stanton cut to the chase and asked straight out what the studio head thought of it. 'You had me at "fish",' came the reply.

Sometimes we work so hard at something that we lose all sight of the fact that it is already good enough, or else is simply not going to work, and that either way it is time to stop and move on. There are four volumes to *Das Kapital* but only the first was printed during Marx's lifetime, and even that was twelve years late. The other volumes (the fourth is sometimes disputed) were put together by Marx co-worker Friedrich Engels from Marx's notes. Marx, it seems, struggled to leave well alone and constantly re-wrote the work from the moment he started. Francis Wheen, one of the most readable of all the commentators on Marx, tells the story that just before the first volume of *Das*

Kapital went to the printers the bearded wonder urged Engels to read a story by Balzac called The Unknown Masterpiece. If it's true, then it's very revealing – this tale concerns a painter called Frenhofer who spends ten years working on a portrait which he expects to revolutionise art. When he finally unveils it to his fellow artists, however, they can't make head or tail of it since it has been painted and repainted out of all recognition. There are many who feel that the convoluted arguments and even more muddled prose of *Das Kapital* represent exactly that failing and it is touching to think that Marx himself may have suspected the same – sufficiently, at least, to nudge his editor and colleague in that direction.

What Frenhofer could have done differently was to introduce some third party advice earlier in the process, and that's still a good tactic today. Get external advice before launching into something lengthy and risky, or when you realise that you're in too deep and failing to progress on something already under way. Don't forget the wisdom of Nemo either. Sometimes you have to accept that while something isn't perfect, it is good enough, and 'good enough' right now may be vastly preferable to 'perfect' at some unspecified point in the future.

HERE'S AN IDEA FOR YOU...

When embarking on a new project decide how you can break it down into manageable steps; set goals for the end of each so you can review before committing to the whole endeavour. The purpose of each review isn't just to see how you're doing – it should help you decide whether or not to drop it or go on.

35 GET INVOLVED IN A SKILLS EXCHANGE

'The price of labour time itself is finally determined by the equation: value of a day's labour = daily value of labour-power. Piece-wage is, therefore, only a modified form of time-wage.'

A skills exchange gets right to the heart of the Marxian ideal of working by avoiding the notion of commodities, re-connecting workers with the importance of their own skills, and re-connecting that with their fellow workers and their community.

DEFINING IDEA...
I have friends in overalls whose friendship I would not swap for the favour of the kings of the world.
~ THOMAS EDISON

The way it works is usually based on either a straight skill swap or a Time Bank system. Skill swaps couldn't be easier and usually work around the idea of a bulletin board in which everybody advertises what they can do for others and what sort of things they would be interested in by way of return. Typical entries would be 'trade English lessons for French' or 'accountancy offered in return for employer liability advice.'

That works well when everyone involved has a skill and a demand that are roughly matched, but it may not be so useful when the demand is more one-sided. For example, plenty of people are interested in a baby-sitter or a gardener, but if the skill they have to offer is teaching Tagalog then they may not find they get the takers they're looking for. Which is where the Time Bank idea comes in.

Time Banks don't deal in money but use time as a currency instead, and usually work on the basis that all workers are equal and all labour equally valuable. You earn a time credit for every hour you spend giving your labour or skills to help others, and then cash it in for a similar amount of time from someone with the muscle or skill that you need. You don't have to spend time credits at once, so you could store them and really let rip on a particularly large job where you'd like the help of a number of labourers at once. There are even systems whereby you can donate your credits to other members as presents or to help out those more needy than yourself. The kind of things typically being traded include gardening, dog walking, ironing, language lessons, computer skills, accountancy, music lessons, reading aloud or shopping. A good Time Bank will start off with a questionnaire that lets you specify what you can offer. Something simple like 'dog walking' needs no explanation but more complex notions like 'tax advice' need to be specified so people can see exactly what your area of expertise is.

Some skills exchanges may also allow you to use money to buy hours if you find you have a shortage of time available to you, but the idea isn't so much about providing a shop front for services as setting up a means of giving and receiving without anyone having to resort to money. That said, there's no doubt that it's also a great way of putting potential clients in touch with those who offer services, so you may also see it as a useful marketing tool for an existing service provider.

HERE'S AN IDEA FOR YOU...

Can't find a skills exchange? Start one. Your own company may be all you need to start offering and receiving skill swaps. It doesn't take a huge amount of technical skill or money to get off the ground. Begin with an open-source bulletin board product and get the ball rolling.

36 GO BACK TO BARTERING

'Therefore, as he [Aristotle] goes on to show, the original form of trade was barter, but with the extension of the latter, there arose the necessity for money. On the discovery of money, barter of necessity developed into [greek: kapelike], into trading in commodities, and this again, in opposition to its original tendency, grew into Chrematistic, into the art of making money.' That's Marx on Aristotle and the birth of trade.

DEFINING IDEA...

What we call 'progress' is the exchange of one nuisance for another nuisance.

– HAVELOCK ELLIS, BRITISH PSYCHOLOGIST

Marx doesn't sound overly fond of barter, but that's because he sees it as an intermediate stage in the oppression of the worker because the worker is creating a surplus value which he then exchanges with another. To Marx barter is just proto-currency: 'The appearance of products as commodities pre-supposes such a development of the social division of labour, that the separation of use-value from exchange-value, a separation which first begins with barter, must already have been completed.'

In fact barter still has a role to play in modern business in the form of barter exchanges that exist as trading platforms for member companies to sell products and services to each other using an internal currency. This isn't just an exercise in exchanging Monopoly money; modern barter can increase sales while improving cash flow and with a trade credit system (as you trade you are paid in credits) you don't have to barter a direct exchange so you can sell to and buy from different partners at the same time. The exchange itself takes care of record keeping, brokering and providing statements of accounts. A commercial exchange makes its money on the side in the form of a marketplace fee, usually a percentage commission on successful transactions.

There are reckoned to be more than 350,000 businesses in the US alone taking part in barter exchange, and more than 400 commercial barter companies serve the global market with two noted industry associations: the National Association of Trade Exchanges (NATE) and the International Reciprocal Trade Association (IRTA).

Don't be surprised if the system becomes even more popular. The idea is traced back to 1934 and the shortage of currency in the wake of the 1929 Wall Street Crash. That inspired the foundation of the first commercial barter system – the Swiss WIR Bank. The WIR bank ('wir' means 'we' in German) was only open to small- and medium-sized enterprises and aimed to keep buying and selling circulating amongst them. The idea certainly took off, and WIR's membership now stands at over 60,000 – exchanging trade to the tune of around 3 billion Swiss Francs. Barter networks not only preserve cash, they help introduce clients to sellers and can often allow both to realise considerable efficiencies and economies by streamlining the purchasing process and the transfer of goods.

If you're looking at a warehouse full of stock, or an empty order book for your services, then maybe it's time to stop thinking about getting out there and selling it, and instead look for a platform that can help you barter it to get the business moving and ensure fluidity in times of limited liquidity.

HERE'S AN IDEA FOR YOU...

Swapping goods isn't just good for cash flow; it's the most efficient way of recycling. That's the thinking behind Freecycle, the online swap shop that has seen its British users double to 1.2 million in the light of the credit crunch. Raid the attic and swap what you find for someone else's unused bicycle.

37 GOING IT ALONE

'We also saw that at first, the subjection of labour to capital was only a formal result of the fact, that the labourer, instead of working for himself, works for and consequently under the capitalist.'

People have been working for the man for as long as there's been a 'man' to work for. But it doesn't have to be that way. You could go out and set up on your own.

Everyone who has ever toiled in an office has thought about working for themselves. Of course, the daydreams tend to revolve around rather idealised pictures in which not only is there no boss, but the work is something you've always wanted to do or else it takes place in a totally stress-free manner with no problems so much as showing their ugly faces.

DEFINING IDEA...
Sexual harassment at work...
is it a problem for the self-employed?
– VICTORIA WOOD, WRITER AND COMEDIAN

The problem is that being self-employed doesn't mean there is no boss – there is a boss, and it's you. The first thing you have to think about, therefore, is just how good a boss you're going to be. Are you going to be a lousy people manager who ends up with the workforce spending most of their time staring out the window or standing in front of an open fridge door? Or will you turn into a monster and make your poor underling slave for long hours and quietly eat into their private lives in the process? Both are surprisingly common.

You're also about to take on a lot of responsibilities that right now your company takes care of, including planning for sick pay, pension, tax and VAT. If you're not putting money aside for tax as you go, then you had better be the favourite prodigy of a particularly rich uncle or else you're in for a nasty surprise when the tax man finally catches up with you.

One really good idea is to go and talk to an accountant before even starting out on your new business. That way not only will you get an idea of your likely tax liability, but you'll also start to think about what can legitimately be deducted from tax as you go – and that may very well re-shape the way you go about your business once you look into how to best handle overheads to minimise costs. It's also a great idea to see an accountant before you even start because they are unromantic individuals and unlikely to see your venture with the same soft focus you do. That means they may well point out gaping holes in your financial planning before you fall through them.

Most governments are keen to help start small businesses and there is a wealth of advice and expertise you can access just by getting in touch with the relevant local authority. Don't forget to do your research either and ensure that there is a market for what you are offering and, where others have gone before you, that you are not simply destined to repeat their mistakes.

HERE'S AN IDEA FOR YOU...

Don't wait to be made redundant or resign in a huff if you're unhappy. Remember the ethical aspect of stealing clients and avoid anything that your current employer could reproach you with, but you run far less risk of a rude awakening if you test the waters of your new life without first burning bridges in the old one.

38 FORM A CO-OPERATIVE

'As the co-operative character of the labour-process becomes more and more marked, so, as a necessary consequence, does our notion of productive labour, and of its agent the productive labourer, become extended.'

Sadly (for Marx, anyway) the workers haven't yet united to shake off their shackles and overthrow the capitalist oppressor. At least not the last bit, because while capitalism may be alive and well, so is the co-operative character of labour – and co-operatives are more common than you might think.

The thinking behind a co-op is that it is a jointly owned and democratically run enterprise in which people unite to help each other realise their aspirations. Unlike non-co-operative businesses, they are not controlled by shareholders or financial investors solely for the pursuit of profit.

DEFINING IDEA...

These concepts of vision and togetherness are only words if we don't live up to them.

~ THEO EPSTEIN, BASEBALL MANAGER

That may sound a little fluffy, but according to the International Co-Operative Alliance co-operatives around the world employ more than 100 million people (that's 20% more than multinationals) and have more than 800 million individual members. Co-operatives may be most associated with fishing, farming and housing, but they also include utilities companies, transport, health and financial services.

In the UK the Co-op went from being a small shop in Lancashire to the UK's largest co-operative (it only takes a £1 share to have a say in the running of the business) with 1.5 million members, 87,000 employees, 10 million customers a week and an annual turnover of over £9 billion from food, healthcare, travel, funeral care and financial services. All of this against a strong background of ethical business.

Co-operatives aren't exempt from the normal rules of business. Just as you can't really live off love and fresh air, you can't really run a company if your business model isn't viable. Any co-operative has to start off by asking if they have a unique selling point that the customer will respond to, and how they will compare with similar businesses that already exist. A co-operative does have the advantage that it doesn't have the relentless shareholder pressure for profits. That alone may make it financially viable, because it can continue to function on margins that might be scorned by mainstream business.

That said, the best co-operatives do make money and can prove extremely efficient precisely because their owners/workers buy into the core values of the business and can see the benefits that it provides for them. In that respect the co-operative is the perfect answer to the problem perceived by Marx that working for a company essentially alienates the labourer from the job he or she does. Because the profits return to the workers, and the running of the business becomes a matter for them, they can identify with their own enterprise and take control of a certain degree of their working destiny. Or, for the cynical, it at least means they get to have a hand in their own exploitation.

HERE'S AN IDEA FOR YOU...

Start your own co-operative. They don't have to be huge or responsible for coffee plantations – they could just be a way of increasing your buying power (get together and get a bulk discount) or claiming a stake in your community. One group of people I know formed a co-op to buy their village pub and keep it open.

39 YOU ARE WHAT YOU DO

'By thus acting on the external world and changing it, he at the same time changes his own nature. He develops his slumbering powers and compels them to act in obedience to his sway.'

Comparing the relatively soulless actions of the factory worker with the (slightly idealised) independent craftsman Marx concludes that we find satisfaction and enrichment through our work by discovering and developing our abilities. Smothering that process by assigning people mechanical jobs alienates them from their own selves and their potential.

DEFINING IDEA...

Nothing builds self-esteem and self-confidence like accomplishment.

~ THOMAS CARLYLE

Our attitudes to work are complex. For most of us work is easier than for any previous generation, and yet we are least likely to identify with it. This is partly because no job carries the security it once had – even the 'safe' careers like banking or accountancy now suffer from redundancy and downsizing – so the idea of a job for life has changed and with it the concept of a career has been re-evaluated. It's increasingly likely, for example, to find people with 'good' jobs featuring healthy salaries, pension packages, company cars – the works – who jack it all in to go travelling or do voluntary work. Work is no longer seen as simply a means of putting food on the table, or a badge that identifies us in society; instead it is expected to help explore and even fulfil our individuality. Of course, that's not always the case and there's nothing like a downturn to focus people's minds back on the 'food on table' element, but in general we can usefully examine our work in the light of Maslow's Hierarchy of Needs.

Back in the 1940s, psychologist Abraham Maslow created a hierarchy, usually represented as a pyramid, of human needs. At the bottom are the basics for survival – food, water, sleep, etc. – followed on a rising scale by security, then friendship and family and then finally into the upper levels of esteem, and finally self-actualisation (things like morality, creativity and spontaneity).

The idea is that you only focus on the higher levels when each lower level is complete. If you don't have food you tend not to worry so much about self-actualisation but as life gets better, and you have security and friendship sorted out, your thoughts turn to needs of esteem – and so on. Maslow felt that educators should aim towards the idea of self-actualising so that individuals are encouraged to be authentic ('be yourself'), to discover a vocation and seek the precious in life, and above all to transcend trifling problems and come to terms with the major issues ('don't sweat the small stuff').

The workers Marx observed didn't have that luxury since they were trapped at the bottom of the period securing basic needs (and probably a certain degree of esteem). Most of us don't have that excuse. So in our own careers we should look beyond the pay scale and think about how much our jobs help us look beyond the trivia of life towards maximising our self-actualisation.

HERE'S AN IDEA FOR YOU...

Write down the things about your job that give you enhanced self-esteem and a sense of recognition from others. Now write down things that give you a sense of personal development, creativity and growth. Not enough in the second list? Time to think about where you're going and what you can do to expand it.

40 BIGGER MAY NOT BE BETTER

'It realises itself now in profit for a few capitalists. The spindles and looms, formerly scattered over the face of the country, are now crowded together in a few great labour-barracks, together with the labourers and the raw material.'

DEFINING IDEA...

In the long history of humankind (and animal kind, too) those who learned to collaborate and improvise most effectively have prevailed.

– CHARLES DARWIN

Marx foresaw the way in which business continually devours itself, with the winners growing ever bigger and the losers either becoming fodder for them or going to the wall. It's an argument that rages today, particularly in the high street where smaller independent shops are being squeezed out of business by the economies of scale, marketing muscle and general economic might of the big retail chains. 'One does not perceive, when looking at the large manufactories and the large farms, that they have originated from the throwing into one of many small centres of production, and have been built up by the expropriation of many small independent producers. Nevertheless, the popular intuition was not at fault. In the time of Mirabeau, the lion of the Revolution, the great manufactories were still called manufactures réunies, workshops thrown into one, as we speak of field thrown into one.'

The unreconstructed capitalist would point out that this is effectively survival of the fittest, an evolution which is driven by consumer demand. As part of their drive to dominate the high street the big retailers have given the consumer wider choice, extended opening hours and lower prices. Show me a disgruntled punter grumbling about the disappearance of the high street grocer and I'll show you someone who does their weekly shop at Tesco regardless of the family fruit shop over the road. Nonetheless, there is also the valid point that the big is better approach doesn't suit everyone. Smaller businesses aren't just quaint; they're more human.

Marx was an admirer of Mirabeau and quotes him at length on the subject of the cottage industry: 'The large workshop (manufacture réunie) will enrich prodigiously one or two entrepreneurs, but the labourers will only be journeymen, paid more or less, and will not have any share in the success of the undertaking. In the discrete workshop (manufacture separée), on the contrary, no one will become rich, but many labourers will be comfortable; the saving and the industrious will be able to amass a little capital, to put by a little for a birth of a child, for an illness, for themselves or their belongings …Discrete workshops, for the most part combined with cultivation of small holdings, are the only free ones.'

Preserving your freedom as a small business doesn't have to mean going head to head with big business (you're not going to win that one) or just giving up and going under. Think about getting together with like-minded businesses. Take the example of farmers' markets, which have been the salvation of many smallholdings. By coming together smallholders have increased their range of products and their appeal to consumers, and so formed a collaborative marketplace in which each benefits the other – while reinforcing the brand value of small suppliers and 'straight from the farm.'

HERE'S AN IDEA FOR YOU...

You don't have to be a smallholder. Swatch was formed by an alliance of high-end Swiss watch manufacturers responding to falling market share. They came up with a cheap and cheerful product that helped save their industry. Would your future be better served by getting together with your rivals and working against the big boys?

41 DOWN WITH DEBT

'When a person gets through all his property, by taking upon himself debts equal to the value of that property, it is clear that his property represents nothing but the sum total of his debts.'

According to the BBC, if you take consumer, corporate and public-sector debt, the ratio of our borrowings in the UK to our annual economic output is a bit over 300%, or over £4000 billion. In short, our country represents nothing but the sum total of our debts. And then some.

DEFINING IDEA...

Blessed are the young, for they shall inherit the national debt.

– HERBERT HOOVER

Debt has for so long been a standard feature of life that many of us, asked if we are in debt, would immediately reply 'no' with a clear conscience since we have stopped even thinking of credit cards, mortgages, or overdrafts as debt – they're simply a convenience of normal life. This may have to change, given the seismic shifts in the global financial markets in which easy and unregulated lending is now seen as one of the key sources of the woes of the world.

Worse, and this is the bit that Karl Marx would have been wringing his hands over, it is the underpaid, exploited but thrifty workers of the Far East who have funded the spending spree in the West. China's £1400 billion in foreign exchange reserves proved irresistible to Western bankers who negotiated deals whereby they borrowed from the East and lent it to those pink round-eyes in the West so they could buy plasma TVs and houses in all the nice postal areas. Hence Zhou Xiaochuan, governor of the Chinese central bank, complaining that 'over-consumption and a high reliance on credit is the cause of the US financial crisis' and that 'as the largest and most important economy in the world, the US should take the initiative to adjust its policies, raise its savings ratio appropriately and reduce its trade and fiscal deficits.' Meaning that effectively the labourer has been screwed again, this time by global capitalism taking money, ironically, from one of the last communist states, and handing it to those wasters in the West.

Now, more than ever, is a good time to take a good long look at your debts, both personal and professional, and try to clear them.

Start with a debt audit – a cold hard look at what you are really borrowing. That means taking off those rose-tinted specs and recognising that a credit card might be called that but it's really a debt card, and those store cards may have seemed like a great idea when you took them out and got a discount, but that was ages ago and have you checked their APR lately? Actually no, you haven't, have you, because almost nobody actually goes back and regularly checks up on the interest they are being charged on their many debts. So now's the time – and while you're at it, don't forget to look into your personal loans, your mortgage, your overdraft and any interest-free lending you took out.

HERE'S AN IDEA FOR YOU...

One of the commonest ways of clearing debts is a consolidation loan, but it's not the best choice. Instead single out the debt with the worst rate (it's probably a credit card). Now pay the minimum on all your other debts until you've paid off bad boy number one.

42 SAVE YOURSELVES

'Accumulate, accumulate! ...save, save, i.e, reconvert the greatest possible portion of surplus-value, or surplus-product into capital! Accumulation for accumulation's sake, production for production's sake: by this formula classical economy expressed the historical mission of the bourgeoisie, and did not for a single instant deceive itself over the birth-throes of wealth.'

DEFINING IDEA...

Always be nice to bankers. Always be nice to pension fund managers. Always be nice to the media. In that order.

– JOHN GOTTI, US GANGSTER

It may sound as if Marx is exhorting us all to be rich, but he's just aping the battle cry of capitalism. He saw the whole thing as a rich man's game in which only the wealthy got wealthier – and if you take a cold look around you at today's world, it's hard to say

he was entirely wrong. If you're reading a business advice book, however, the chances are that you're not exactly toiling at the coal face (not since most mines closed, anyway) and instead you have a small store of savings that you'd like to turn into a much larger store. Which means shares, savings and pensions. If you're smart, you've probably spread your accumulated assets across all three.

Shares have taken a battering. Marx wouldn't have batted an eyelid at that, since one thing he points out repeatedly is that capitalism isn't a steady progression but a repetitive cycle of good times and bad, occasionally punctuated with disastrous crashes. We tend to forget that, however, and wail about falling share prices. Andy Hornby, former chief executive of HBOS, told the UK parliament that he hadn't taken a bonus in the previous year, taking it in shares instead. Following the banking crisis he exclaimed that 'I've lost considerably more money than I've been paid'. The poor dear. Not only does that show just how out of touch he is with the public but it's also deceptive, since a short-term dip in a share's price is not really a problem if you have enough wealth to wait it out and watch prices rally. Over a ten-year period equities will still tend to rise, even if that decade includes a depression. The problem will be for those whose savings were linked to share prices but were only realised at the share value's nadir. If you were thinking of cashing in a pension in those circumstances, you'd be best advised to hold off if possible, since it would return a frighteningly poor rate. Not only that, but the slump in sterling would mean you couldn't run off to live it up in Marbella since sterling's exchange rate dropped against everything from the Euro to the Mongolian Tögrög.

If you're not about to retire, then private pensions are still a fair bet because of the associated tax breaks and top-ups, but be careful about putting it all in one scheme; financial institutions aren't as bulletproof as we once thought. Investments such as property are still an option, as are shares if you're in it for the long term, but the sensible approach is, above all, to spread your risk across different institutions and markets.

HERE'S AN IDEA FOR YOU...

Pensions have downsides – cash is locked away, they're inflexible, you're stuck with the annuity you get when you cash them in, and much of the value is lost if you die shortly after retiring. So consider ISAs as well, if you're a UK tax payer. They're limited in value but enjoy similar tax breaks and a great deal more flexibility.

43 NEW CAPITALISM

Marx talks excitedly about '...*the power of the State, the concentrated and organised force of society, to hasten, hot-house fashion, the process of transformation of the feudal mode of production into the capitalist mode, and to shorten the transition. Force is the midwife of every old society pregnant with a new one. It is itself an economic power*'.

DEFINING IDEA...

Capitalism has destroyed our belief in any effective power but that of self interest backed by force.
~ GEORGE BERNARD SHAW

Force has taken a bit of a turn of late with the banking crisis and the realisation that Western society has been borrowing beyond its means and lending against the value of assets which have proved worthless. The net result of that, notably in the UK and US, is that those investment banks, the standard bearers and shock troops of capitalism, found themselves perilously short of ready cash and staring into the gulf of total collapse. At which point they cheerfully forgot all those free-market mantras about non-interference from the state and turned to the taxpayer, bleating for help. It's reckoned that the UK taxpayer has forked out around £600 billion to prop up the banking system; in the US it's more than nine times that. Nor is that the end of it; there is still talk of further intervention and possibly even total nationalisation for the high street banks.

Karl's whiskers would have been positively a-wobble with chuckles. Either that or he'd have been hopping from one foot to another while indulging in an orgy of finger wagging and 'I told you so'.

There is just one glimmer of good news in all this. Through the 80s and 90s we saw the investment bankers building power – greed was good and no government, not even a supposedly socialist one, was going to stand in the way of the great cash cows of capitalism. In those circumstances, the banks benefited from 'the concentrated and organised force of society, to hasten, hot-house fashion, the process of transformation'.

Now, however, the tide has turned and taxpayers and their governments are not likely to be so forgiving of the financial sector's excesses. Or as Robert Peston, the BBC's Business Editor, says of the banks: 'Their survival as institutions now wholly depends on the goodwill of governments and taxpayers around the world. From Australia, to South Korea, to Germany, France, the UK and the US – inter alia – taxpayers' financial support for the banking system is now equivalent to more than one quarter of global GDP, or more than £9000 billion…So if we've witnessed a semi-permanent nationalisation of the banking system and will soon see significant taxpayer support for real companies in the real economy, then our banks and private-sector companies will have to work much harder to sustain the goodwill of those who are keeping them alive: millions and millions of taxpayers.'

Which means that the watchwords for the near future are likely to be transparency and responsibility. Checks and balances will be demanded and 'greed is good' will have to be replaced with cautious capitalism.

HERE'S AN IDEA FOR YOU…

The banking crisis has shown the folly of ignoring whistleblowers. Set up your own anonymous whistleblowing channel – a suggestions box is one idea but a bulletin board system with potential for anonymous log-on is better – and give someone the responsibility to check it to weed out genuine wrongdoing.

44 OVERDOING IT

'Hence in antiquity over-work becomes horrible only when the object is to obtain exchange-value in its specific independent money-form; in the production of gold and silver. Compulsory working to death is here the recognised form of over-work.'

DEFINING IDEA...

Stress is an ignorant state. It believes that everything is an emergency. Nothing is that important. Just lie down.
~ NATALIE GOLDBERG, ZEN AUTHOR

Compulsory working to death has gone out of fashion in modern business but working your way to a shorter lifespan is pretty much the norm when you take stress into account. I doubt that Karl was thinking about those pulling a ten-hour day at the desk when he wrote of the horrors of overwork, but it won't sound so unfamiliar to the average desk jockey.

'But as soon as people, whose production still moves within the lower forms of slave-labour, corvée-labour, &c., are drawn into the whirlpool of an international market dominated by the capitalistic mode of production, the sale of their products for export becoming their principal interest, the civilised horrors of over-work are grafted on the barbaric horrors of slavery, serfdom, etc.'

In Japanese there is a term for working yourself to death – karoshi. Chinese newspapers call death by overwork guolaosi. In the UK we call it 'mustn't grumble'. The protestant work ethic has a lot to answer for.

In her book Willing Slaves: How the Overwork Culture is Ruling Our Lives, Madeleine Bunting reveals that not only do Brits tend to work more hours than anyone else in Europe, but the number of people working over 48 hours has more than doubled since 1998, from 10% to 26%. More than that, 65% of us don't take a lunch hour (the average is now less than half that) and even then it's usually spent at the workstation rather than in the local park. We don't even take our holiday entitlement – it's estimated that only 44% of workers use up their full entitlement to annual leave.

All of which takes its toll. Work stress results in headaches, upset stomachs, an overflow of tensions with friends and family, sleeplessness and burnout. High stress levels can cause or exacerbate heart disease, weight gain, asthma, high blood pressure, ulcers and migraines. It can also damage the health of your businesses. The Health and Safety Executive's 2006/07 survey of self-reported work-related illness revealed that 13.8 million working days were lost to work-related stress, depression and anxiety, and that each case of work-related stress, depression or anxiety-related ill health led to an average of 30.2 working days lost – costing the economy over £530 million.

Dealing with work stress starts now and it starts with you. Stress busting can be as simple as smiling and ensuring you get enough sleep, exercise and a balanced diet. Finding a means to relax that works for you (meditation, walking, listening to music, etc.), and taking care of not only your own work – life balance but also that of those around you are also key. Don't forget that stress is contagious, so if your co-workers are stressing out, you will be too. Finally, if it really is getting too much don't be afraid to seek help.

HERE'S AN IDEA FOR YOU...

The first step in tackling stress from overwork is acknowledging it in yourself and in others. Does your company have a stress policy, defining stress at work, giving the symptoms so it can be recognised, and setting out what management and individuals can do about it? No? Set one up.

45 YOU WANT TO THINK OUTSIDE THE BOX – LEARN FROM OUTSIDE THE BOX

'Originally, Political Economy was studied by philosophers like Hobbes, Locke, Hume; by businessmen and statesmen, like Thomas More, Temple, Sully, De Witt, North, Law, Vanderlint, Cantillon, Franklin; and especially, and with the greatest success, by medical men like Petty, Barbon, Mandeville, Quesnay.'

DEFINING IDEA...

Politicians should read science fiction, not westerns and detective stories.

~ ARTHUR C. CLARKE
(WHO WROTE SCIENCE FICTION, AS IT HAPPENS)

Marx was a regular in the old British Museum Reading Room and in his search for an understanding of the capitalist system and its exploitation of the worker he read, reasonably enough, a wide range of political economists, businessmen and statesmen. As well as those mentioned above, he also delved deeply into the writings of French socialists such as Fourier, Saint-Simon and Proudhon and economists such as Hobbs, Franklin and Smith. What might be less obvious is the amount of research he put into the Greek philosophy of Democritus and Epicurus. Aristotle, and in particular his thinking on slavery and on Nicomachean Ethics, also plays a major part as an influence on Marx's assessment of the movement of money and society.

His range of influences includes a star-studded cast of unexpected bit players. As Francis Wheen observes in *Marx's Das Kapital – A Biography*: 'The first volume of Das Kapital yielded quotations from the Bible, Shakespeare, Goethe, Milton, Voltaire, Homer, Balzac, Dante, Schiller, Sophocles, Plato,

Thucydides, Xenophon, Defoe, Cervantes, Dryden, Heine, Virgil, Juvenal, Horace, Thomas More, Samuel Butler – as well as allusions to horror tales, English romantic novels, popular ballads, songs and jingles, melodrama and farce, myths and proverbs.'

Marx developed the habit of taking notes from everything he read when he was at university, copying out all the bits that caught his magpie eye and mentally cross-referencing them with each other. While studying the philosophy of law, he took the time to teach himself about the history of art, to learn English and Italian, and to translate classics such as Tacitus' Germania and Aristotle's Rhetoric. In particular, he records that he relished his reading of Reimarus, noting that he 'spent a good deal of time on Reimarus, to whose book on the artistic instincts of animals I applied my mind with delight'.

What's interesting about his singling out of Reimarus is that Hermann Samuel Reimarus was a philosopher whose principal point was that if you wanted a better understanding of God and the working of the world then you should study his works in the form of nature, rather than rely on religious writings and supposed revelations of the truth to selected individuals. In short, put the manual down and look at what's actually in front of you.

Marx would have been an odd figure, spouting quotations and poetry as he walked on Hampstead Heath with his family, but in his eclectic and all-encompassing reading he was espousing a philosophy that you don't learn about your subject from the revelations of a select few but from observing ecosystems and ethics in motion instead.

HERE'S AN IDEA FOR YOU...

What this book tries to demonstrate is that even capitalists can learn from Marx and his observations. Try putting aside the business books for a moment and cast your net wider than modern management methodology – consider how philosophy, ethics and even natural sciences can be applied to your line of work.

46 PAY WHAT YOU WANT

'The value of a commodity is expressed in its price before it goes into circulation, and is therefore a precedent condition of circulation, not its result.'

Unless, of course, you don't fix a price and instead let people pay what they want for something. 'Pay What You Want' schemes range from the genuinely generous to the pure publicity stunt, but as conventional economics are challenged and the credit crunch eats the rule book we're going to be seeing a lot more of them.

DEFINING IDEA...

I don't want money. It is only people who pay their bills who want that, and I never pay mine.
~ OSCAR WILDE

A smart restaurant in London has been grabbing headlines (at least on the entertainment pages) by offering a 'pay what you like scheme' for meals. The Little Bay restaurant in Farringdon has launched a 'pay what you think it's worth' month to entice the frugal and fearful to splash out on a credit-crunch lunch. Owner Peter Ilic has said that 'It just seemed the right thing to do with everyone under the cosh and feeling pretty miserable…we have seen so many more City folk coming into the restaurant lately looking for a better value lunch'. A nice bit of publicity, you might think, and you'd be right, although the owner is also confident that he won't end up out of pocket, not least since it's not the first time he's done this – back in 1985 he ran a restaurant in Finchley on the same basis for two years.

The Pay What You Want approach got a lot of coverage when Radiohead released their album In Rainbows on a Pay What You Want download basis.

Clicking on the checkout basket sign for a price on the website brought up the message 'It's Up To You'. Click it again and it says 'It's Really Up To You', and, yes, that does include the option to pay nothing at all.

The trend is popping up elsewhere as a result of the economic downturn. An Ibis hotel, Ibis Singapore on Bencoolen, allows guests to log on to a website – www.paywhatyouwant.com.sg – and bid for what you want to pay. MIDEM, one of the world's biggest music conferences, has partnered with a real estate company in Cannes, France to offer forty apartments in the city during the conference at whatever price a MIDEM visitor wants to pay. Good magazine has offered a subscription service that lets customers pay anything for a copy as long as it's over a dollar (though pay $20 or more and you also get invited to their parties).

What's more interesting, however, is that this approach isn't just a flash in the pan response to desperate times. In Berlin, a Pay What You Want deal has been the norm in a number of bars for more than a decade now – and they're still doing business. Jürgen Stumpf's three bars started out on Pay What You Want because initially the fledgling owners simply didn't know what to charge. The system has endured, however, and now continues after 8 p.m. most nights.

HERE'S AN IDEA FOR YOU...

Thinking of introducing Pay What You What into your marketing mix? Don't forget that while the existence of the business is a tribute to human honesty, many schemes have ensured their survival by letting people know what others paid and, where possible, having payment done face to face with a real live human being.

47 DON'T KEEP IT TO YOURSELF

'This antagonism between the quantitative limits of money and its qualitative boundlessness, continually acts as a spur to the hoarder in his Sisyphus-like labour of accumulating. It is with him as it is with a conqueror who sees in every new country annexed, only a new boundary.'

DEFINING IDEA...

No man will make a great leader who wants to do it all himself, or to get all the credit for doing it.

~ ANDREW CARNEGIE

Hoarding, Marx points out, is a primitive response to the appreciation of the capitalist system and the possibility of accumulating. 'To a barbarian owner of commodities, and even to a West-European peasant, value is the same as value-form, and therefore to him the increase in his hoard of gold and silver is an increase in value.' The more you have, the more you want and the more pain it costs you to let it go. Hoarding, however, can actually reduce the capitalist's ability to accumulate because without the speculation, consumption and circulation the system collapses. 'We have seen how, along with the continual fluctuations in the extent and rapidity of the circulation of commodities and in their prices, the quantity of money current unceasingly ebbs and flows.'

Purely in terms of money, that point has been made very forcibly by the financial situation of 2008–9 in which 'liquidity' has fast become the watchword of banks, and in turn the general business population has rounded on those banks and accused them of hoarding money and thus slowing or preventing any economic recovery. You don't have to be a rampant Keynesian to see that if you don't share it around the whole system grinds to a halt.

What's often missed in all this, however, is that the same is just as true for intellectual capital. For the modern manager to accrue success they must stop hoarding it, and learn to spend it wisely, speculating to accumulate more success from the people they work with. Helping others to learn and thrive is all part of good management, and the way to do that is to focus on noticing and praising success in others.

Time to consider being a mentor. A mentor can be a number of things, but the commonest understanding is someone with considerable entrepreneurial or management experience who decides to make that available to protégés or clients. That can be done for financial reward through mentoring agencies which are run like consultancies, but often it is done mainly as a means of giving something back and to stay fresh with (someone else's) current business dilemmas. In the UK, the chancellor Alistair Darling recently called on entrepreneurs to give more back to the next generation and the popularity of entrepreneur TV shows such as Dragons' Den has made more and more would-be entrepreneurs aware that they can do with the help.

So why be selfish about it? Encouraging success is a success in its own right, and the more you can share your experience and know-how the more you can cultivate a culture of growth around you. Hoarding just leads to stagnation; sharing can help to keep your skills and sense of self-worth fresh.

HERE'S AN IDEA FOR YOU...

Mentoring isn't just about high-powered entrepreneurs. There is a need for mentors to work with kids, with refugees, with digital have-nots and with other businesspeople. For an idea of the range of mentoring skills in demand take a look at www.timebank.org.uk/mentor.

48 FREEDOM OF ASSEMBLY

'*During the very first storms of the revolution, the French bourgeoisie dared to take away from the workers the right of association but just acquired. By a decree of 14 June 1791, they declared all coalition of the workers as "an attempt against liberty and the declaration of the rights of man," punishable by a fine of 500 livres, together with deprivation of the rights of an active citizen for one year.*'

DEFINING IDEA...

Those who desire to give up freedom in order to gain security will not have, nor do they deserve, either one.

– BENJAMIN FRANKLIN

Terms like 'freedom of assembly' and 'collective bargaining' sound oddly dated to the modern ear. For some people they may bring to mind 1970s union stereotypes with images of grumpy blue-collar workers getting together to grumble about management over a cheese sandwich and a bottle of beer. Since freedom of assembly has largely been accepted in the Western world, it is hard to remember that it was once a hard-fought-for freedom and one which is still often under attack.

Marx observes that the ban on freedom of association (and thus unions) lasted an astonishingly long time, and for a good reason: 'This law which, by means of State compulsion, confined the struggle between capital and labour within limits comfortable for capital, has outlived revolutions and changes of dynasties. Even the Reign of Terror left it untouched. It was but quite recently struck out of the Penal Code. Nothing is more characteristic than the pretext for this bourgeois coup d'état. "Granting," says Chapelier, the reporter of the

Select Committee on this law, "that wages ought to be a little higher than they are, …that they ought to be high enough for him that receives them, to be free from that state of absolute dependence due to the want of the necessaries of life, and which is almost that of slavery," yet the workers must not be allowed to come to any understanding about their own interests, nor to act in common and thereby lessen their "absolute dependence, which is almost that of slavery.""

In short, the whole point of assembly and collective action is that it can raise the worker above the level of slavery, but for capital to truly have the whip hand it is best outlawed so that individuals can be individually dealt with – the classic approach of divide and conquer. In the developed world, the freedom of assembly and association is enshrined in law (notably Article 12 of the Charter of Fundamental Rights of the European Union).

With the general decline in unionisation it is often forgotten, however, that in the modern workplace the presence of unions can be good for a business – it's not all about confrontation. Instead unions can make it easier to help with communication, organisation, training and morale. Importantly they have a key role to play in the dimension of corporate social responsibility which, as we saw earlier, is likely to grow in significance in the new capitalism.

HERE'S AN IDEA FOR YOU…

So you've encouraged unionisation in your own workplace as a means of connecting with the workforce. But have you checked that your suppliers in other countries allow freedom of assembly? As the demands for transparency and accountability grow, the pressure is on to look beyond your own premises and scrutinise every other business you influence.

49 KAIZEN

'The additional capitals formed in the normal course of accumulation serve particularly as vehicles for the exploitation of new inventions and discoveries, and industrial improvements in general.'

DEFINING IDEA...

Excellent firms don't believe in excellence – only in constant improvement and constant change.

– TOM PETERS,
AUTHOR OF IN SEARCH OF EXCELLENCE

For Marx, the nature of industry was one of continuous improvement but, as he saw it, that improvement only took the form of perfecting the machinery with a view to further reducing the manual labour required and thus rendering the worker surplus to requirements. 'But in time the old capital also reaches the moment of renewal from top to toe, when it sheds its skin and is reborn like the others in a perfected technical form, in which a smaller quantity of labour will suffice to set in motion a larger quantity of machinery and raw materials.'

In the tough times of Victorian industry there was little thought for making the worker's lot better, let alone considering that the workers themselves might have it in their power to improve processes, conditions and their own degree of satisfaction. What Marx didn't foresee was that more sophisticated and sensitive management could end up with the workers not only increasing productivity for the company, but also taking pride in the fact and thus working to end the sense of alienation from their own roles that Marx saw as an inevitable part of capitalism.

'Kaizen' comes from the Japanese terms for change (kai) and to become good (zen) and is usually interpreted as a process of continual improvement of processes. It is usually associated with companies such as Honda, Suzuki and particularly Nippon Steel which began the process of kaizen in the early 1960s. Kaizen wasn't always called that and it is revealing that the term originally used was 'jishu kanri' (self-management) which gives a flavour of the approach. Essentially, it relies on teams being responsible for their output and so coming up with suggestions themselves for making it better. Unfortunately that has led to it being mistaken for a kind of management free lunch in which workers do all the thinking as if the process was no more than a suggestion box.

Where kaizen has proved most effective it has been a process initiated by workers but managed systematically. In Nippon Steel, for example, it takes the form of a mixture of voluntary, paid and mandatory elements. As an example, a study at Nippon Steel revealed that official jishu kanri meetings accounted for five hours a week of worker time, which was paid, but which then prompted between two and eight hours a week of informal discussion amongst workers, often during lunch breaks or after work. This unpaid and voluntary kaizen work was, however, ultimately rewarded in the form of performance-related bonuses. Another point to note is that kaizen helped engender a powerful team spirit with teams competing with each other within plants to come up with the best performance increases. In some cases that even led to teams dismantling improved machine settings at the end of shifts to keep them secret from each other.

HERE'S AN IDEA FOR YOU...

Kaizen can be applied to almost any line of business as long as you recognise the four key principles: team spirit, an understanding of efficiency in the process, feedback and continuous evolution. Think how well your company or department rates on each and what you could do to make each one work better.

50 LUNCH 'N' LEARN

'Since, before entering on the process, his own labour has already been alienated from himself by the sale of his labour-power, has been appropriated by the capitalist and incorporated with capital, it must, during the process, be realised in a product that does not belong to him.'

DEFINING IDEA...

A business has to be involving, it has to be fun, and it has to exercise your creative instincts.

– RICHARD BRANSON

For Marx the alienation imposed by the capitalist system is fourfold. 'Firstly, workers, from the moment they are taken from the rural environment of growing food, are alienated from the product of their labour and by implication from the natural world. Secondly, they are alienated from the labour process itself because the division of labour reduced the craft involved and makes man an adjunct to the machine. Thirdly, the individual worker is alienated from his own nature since he is a worker first, a person second; furthermore his limited work role serves to stifle his development. Fourthly, and as a direct result of the other forms of alienation, man is alienated from his own humanity and as a result loses contact with his fellow man.'

You don't have to be a full-on Marxist to appreciate that a lot of this is demonstrably true and that a joyless job in a soulless workplace really isn't going to make Jack a fulfilled boy. There again you probably aren't about to tear down the capitalist system, so how can you make a difference that might help reduce or remove those alienating trends?

This is where a constructive company culture comes in. Company culture isn't going to solve everything but it can go a long way towards reconstructing the links between workers and between workers and the ultimate goal of the company itself. The basics for good culture are:

• **Orientation** Give people a clear idea of what the company stands for, what it aims for and how it is going to get there.

• **Training** Offer training that combines information and motivation and allow employees to suggest their own training goals as well as being given a suggested curriculum.

• **Communication** Corporate communication is so often a one-way thing, when in truth it should involve constant dialogue using every mechanism possible.

• **Recognition and reward** If good behaviour goes unnoticed it will be replaced by jobsworth stagnation and that helps precisely nobody.

So instigate a Lunch 'n' Learn programme. In any company beyond a certain size, nobody really understands what the different divisions do and that can lead to apathy, disunity and negativity. So have people prepare informal presentations to introduce themselves, their department, their work, their favourite things and their headaches to their co-workers. Lay on some sandwiches and invite everybody in turn to explain to everybody else what it is they really do and how they just might be able to help each other: if it helps to humanise a company, it's a step in the right direction.

HERE'S AN IDEA FOR YOU...

Smart companies offer their best Lunch 'n' Learn presentations to other companies – clients, colleagues and even rivals. If it helps your business ecosystem to understand you, and in the process you can impress them with your expertise and friendliness, then you will build your brand, attract business and covertly recruit wherever you go.

51 YOU ARE WHAT YOU CONSUME

'Man always has been, and must still be a consumer, both before and while he is producing.'

You may be a producer, a manager or a labourer but whatever you are, you are most certainly a consumer. 'Whatever the form of the process of production in a society, it must be a continuous process, must continue to go periodically through the same phases. A society can no more cease to produce than it can cease to consume. When viewed, therefore, as a connected whole, and as flowing on with incessant renewal, every social process of production is, at the same time, a process of reproduction.'

More importantly, Marx points out that the force of capitalism is a movement of forces so that the worker, having left the countryside to seek work, is now forced to consume products since he cannot himself grow food or make his own goods. This perpetuates the cycle and each worker ensures the exploitation of the next.

These days you may not see yourself as the exploiter or exploited while hovering by the deli counter, but your own personal impact as a consumer is undeniable and exploitation still exists in the system. Which is why so many consumers are starting to ask about the ethical dimension of their shopping baskets.

The recession may be hitting, the credit may be well and truly crunched, and the downturn may be being rebranded as a nosedive but one of the interesting things about the consumer reaction to the crash is that the rise in ethical consumerism is predicted to survive. Every year the Co-operative Bank publishes a report into green spending – a barometer of ethical consumerism in the UK. Despite the fact that 2008 was the year in which consumer consumption dried up, the overall ethical market in the UK was worth £35.5 billion and every household in the UK spent £707 in line with their ethical values, up from £630 in 2006. To put that in perspective, ethical consumption is still (free range) chicken feed compared to the annual consumer spend of more than £600 billion, but growth in areas like Fairtrade goods and organic food was up 14%. It seems we prefer to shop with our conscience even when we're cost conscious.

The same story emerges from the Boston Consulting Group's report *Capturing the Green Advantage for Consumer Companies*. In the report the company surveyed 9000 adults in nine countries, and found that 34% of Europeans said they would continue to look for and purchase green products, while 32% of US consumers said the same.

Of course, it remains to be seen whether people continue to buy costly organic produce when they're truly running short on cash. The flip side is that when those ethical consumers go to cheap fast food outlets instead of restaurants, or buy from brand names instead of small suppliers, they may well take their ethical concerns into markets not previously associated with them. Look out for more high street suppliers making ethical promises.

HERE'S AN IDEA FOR YOU...

Consuming less and better is only part of the picture – in order to make a difference you have to campaign more. This can be as simple as letting people know what you buy and why. There's no point boycotting something unless you also take the time to let the organisation you're boycotting know what you're doing.

52 POWER UP

'They must be conscious that much bodily and mental pain has thus been inflicted upon them from causes for which they were in no way answerable; to which, had it been in their power, they would have in no way consented; and against which they were powerless to struggle.'

DEFINING IDEA...

Those who do not move, do not notice their chains.

~ ROSA LUXEMBURG,
MARXIST REVOLUTIONARY

Marx is talking about labourers under the 'gang' system, but the idea of the worker being powerless to struggle is one that runs throughout *Das Kapital*. Marx points out that inequality is inherent in the system since the capitalist can choose not to hire, but the worker – once transplanted from the land, self-sufficiency and status as an independent craftsman – has no option not to work. He must work to survive and can't hold off until wages go up or conditions improve. It's a grim picture and one that plays out to this day in the poorer parts of the world and amongst the most powerless communities of the West.

Chances are, though, that anyone who has this book in their hand doesn't realistically fall into that category. Instead we're of the privileged and educated group who can (largely) pick and choose where and how to work. Our concerns are more likely to include promotions and career paths than the fears of starving or being worked to death on an assembly line. So the challenge now is to realise that power and be sure that we are making the most of the chances that we, unlike the workers Marx observed, have been given.

Ask yourself if you are doing what you want to do. Do you even know why you're doing what you're doing? To pay the bills? Really? Not good enough. It's time to power up because we've all come a long way and you're doing no favours to anyone if you don't make the most of the freedom you have.

Firstly define your purpose. What motivates you? What are your goals? What steps will it take to get to them? Don't be afraid to start with the big goals but make sure you break them down into the steps it takes to get there. Tim Wright, a consultant in creativity, gives a presentation in which he challenges the audience to consider where they want to go. He illustrates it with his own goal – playing golf on the moon with David Bowie. Having started at that extreme he then shows how to break down the goal into its stepping-stone goals such as learning to play golf (not so tough), getting to be friends with David Bowie (tougher, but feasible if approached through the right channels) and finally getting to the moon. This last one would appear insurmountable, but as space tourism looks set to become a reality over the next few years even this now has stepping stones to get there. The point is not to allow the day to day to take away your ability to realise your potential. If we struggle powerlessly it's nobody's fault but our own.

HERE'S AN IDEA FOR YOU...

Write your own mission statement. This shouldn't be an exercise in smooth-talking gibberish, but a genuine statement of intent about what you want to do and how you aim to go about it. Store it somewhere (in your diary, as a file on your desktop) where you can and will see and remember it regularly.

INDEX